You Can Change Your Life Any Time You Want

Robin Sieger

arrow books

Published by Arrow in 2005

1 3 5 7 9 10 8 6 4 2

Copyright © Robin Sieger 2005

First published in the United Kingdom by Arrow in 2005

Arrow
The Random House Group Limited
20 Vauxhall Bridge Road, London SW1V 2SA

Random House Australia (Pty) Limited
20 Alfred Street, Milsons Point, Sydney
New South Wales 2061, Australia

Random House New Zealand Limited
18 Poland Road, Glenfield
Auckland 10, New Zealand

Random House (Pty) Limited
Endulini, 5a Jubilee RoadParktown 2193, South Africa

The Random House Group Limited Reg. No. 954009

www.randomhouse.co.uk

A CIP catalogue record for this book is available from the British Library

Papers used by Random House are natural, recylcable products made from
wood grown in sustainable forests. The manufacturing processes conform
to the environmental regulations of the country of origin

Typeset by SX Composing DTP, Rayleigh, Essex
Printed and bound in Great Britain by
Mackays of Chatham Ltd, Chatham, Kent

ISBN 0 09 947668 1

To my mother Dorothy,
who taught me I could do anything I put my mind to,
and my sisters Louise, Libby, Hilary, Lucie, and Julie
for being such wonderful fun

ACKNOWLEDGEMENTS

At the risk of giving a gushing Oscar style thank-you address, I would like to thank a few people who played a part in the creation of this manuscript. My friend Pat Campbell who read the manuscript over and over again, with only words of encouragement, and suggestions to give clarity. To my agent Abner Stein for his wisdom, and Max Eilenberg for endless cups of tea, to Clare Smith my editor at Arrow for her commitment and endless enthusiasm. To Ash Latif and Lucy Main for their timely support as the deadline loomed.

That's it, to all of you a very big thank you.

CONTENTS

Introduction   The Big Question   ix
How To Use This Book   xiii

Part 1   **Things You Need To Consider**   1
Chapter 1   Just . . . Think!   3
Chapter 2   The Starting Point   14
Chapter 3   Who Do You Think You Are?   23
Chapter 4   Do Your Best To Do Your Best   31
Chapter 5   Don't 'Want' – Determine   35
Chapter 6   Get A Plan – Then Make It Happen   40

Part 2   **Things You Need To Know**   45
Chapter 1   Beliefs   47
Chapter 2   Goals   61
Chapter 3   Action   73
Chapter 4   Attitude   85
Chapter 5   Persistence   95
Chapter 6   Fear   105
Chapter 7   Failure   115
Chapter 8   Honesty   123
Chapter 9   Living In The Present   132
Chapter 10   Patience   143
Chapter 11   Humility   152

Chapter 12   Love   158
Chapter 13   Motivation   170
Chapter 14   Happiness   180
Chapter 15   You Absolutely Need A Plan   192
Chapter 16   Your Life   202
Chapter 17   And Finally . . .   209

Part 3   Things You Need To Do   211
How To Use Part 3   213
The Visualisation Technique   217
Exercise 1   Take Stock   222
Exercise 2   Behaviours   225
Exercise 3   Commitment   229
Exercise 4   Habit Busting   231
Exercise 5   Facing Up To Fear   233
Exercise 6   The Inner Coach – Self-Talk   235
Exercise 7   Setting Meaningful Goals   238
Exercise 8   Creating Your Plan For Success   240
Conclusion   When The Going Gets Tough,
              Remember . . .   243

INTRODUCTION

THE BIG QUESTION

Imagine you are 102 years of age. You have not been too well since you fell off your trampoline some weeks earlier and you are lying in a hospital bed. Your loved ones surround you fondly reminiscing, suddenly a nurse announces that you have visitors some young people who have travelled a long way and are very keen to see you. You've never met any of them before but they know all about you – because of your life achievements. They apologise immediately for bothering you. Then, without giving you a chance even to offer them a cup of herbal tea, one asks a question that has obviously been puzzling them all for a long time, 'What advice would you give to help me be successful in both my business and personal life?' You are delighted to be able to answer this question. Smiling that wise old smile you spent hours perfecting you take a deep breath and gather your thoughts. Oh no – at that exact moment your heart stops. You realise you only have one last lungful of air left, and you desperately want to help this person. So here is the dilemma – what single piece of advice would you give them? If you could give somebody only one piece of advice in life to help them find true success, true happiness, meaning and joy, what would it be?

My piece of advice, I always used to believe, would be simply to tell people to do what they love. Which is all good and fine, but as I thought about it more, I realised there were some other things I would really want to add. I would want to tell people never to give up on their dreams. I would want to tell them to believe in themselves, and to be positive, and to love unconditionally, and to help others, for all these are part of true success in life. As my list of golden death-bed wisdom became longer and longer, it eventually became the foundation of this book. The book is a sharing of my philosophy about what I believe is essential to live a full and happy life. I believe whoever you are and whatever your situation you will find resonance here, that will help you change your life, if you want to.

Life begins when we are dangled upside down by someone, who – we trust – knows what they are doing: they smack our bottom, encouraging us to take our very first breath. Thereafter continue breathing until, at some point in the distant future, we take our last breath, at which point, according to the films I have seen, somebody says in a sombre tone, 'They're gone,' and then gently closes our eyes, if we forgot to do so first.

Our lives are journeys from our birth to our death. That sounds a bit bleak, and so it is, if the death bit is all you think about. I would rather we gave all our attention to the bit in between. We do not like to talk about our mortality but I think it is sometimes good to reflect upon the fact that we have only one life. At the end of that life, when you look back, what do you want to see? What is the view going to be like? I sincerely hope that it is one of joy and happiness, of having experienced a full life, of having achieved wonderful heights of personal success. I think it would be a great sadness if by contrast we look back and can only regret the things we did not do.

Over the past years I have spoken to many people about what their passion is, about what they would most like to get out of life, if anything was possible. The next question I ask is, why they are not doing it. The answer, all too often, is an endless list of reasons and excuses. Are you like that? Do you wish for something more? Do you really want to do something about it? This book is written to encourage you, to inspire you and to guide you.

You really can change your life any day you want, but only if you change the way you think. Changing the way you think is the theme that will run throughout the entire book. The way you think impacts on what you believe; what you believe impacts on how you behave; how you behave impacts on how you perform; and your performance will impact on what you achieve.

I want you to realise too that your life is not predestined, it is not written in the stars. It is written by you. Your life is a book of blank pages. Only all too late do most of us realise that we are the authors of that book, and that whatever we choose to write in it we can achieve. We have one life, full of endless possibilities. It may be a cliché to say that today is the first day of the rest of your life; none the less, it is true. And right now, if you choose, you can change your life and live your dreams. The reason so few people achieve the success they seek is because they are limited by their assumptions. They make assumptions about themselves, they make assumptions about their potential and they make assumptions about other people. Their assumptions are based on what they believe to be true.

So what do you believe to be true about you? We will explore this and other issues in this book. There are hundreds of volumes written about personal development, and no one-size-fits-all philosophy will make things change. There are no secret techniques here that you need to learn, but there are things you need to consider. We are all at different stages in our lives, and while for some, one chapter may be the missing part of a jigsaw, for others, every chapter may have resonance and be of assistance.

Since *Natural Born Winners* was first published I have often been asked what my seven principles of success are based on, and what experiences, philosophy and beliefs lie behind the idea that success is achievable by everyone. It is as a result of these many conversations that this book came about. It is written to enable you to really change your life. It is not prescriptive, instructing you to do this or that. It expresses my own beliefs that have inspired, encouraged and helped me in my own journey through life. I believe they will help you too.

Life is a journey, and like all journeys we need to start with a destination in mind to inspire us. In our lives we must determine where it is we want to go, otherwise we will end up where the wind blows us. Each chapter in this book has a destination, a common purpose. I want it to stimulate you to think, and I want the thinking to stimulate you to take action. I want the action to inspire you to live the life you dreamt of as a child. It is my wish that you discover your own greatness and become the person that deep down inside you felt you always wanted to be. I want you to find your success and joy in your life.

Somebody once told me, 'We were born with all the tools we need to succeed', and then added, 'Unfortunately, we didn't come with a set of instructions'. So I wrote this handbook, in the hope that it can help you.

HOW TO USE THIS BOOK

Part 1   Things You Need To Consider

Part 2   Things You Need To Know

Part 3   Things You Need To Do

Part I has been written as though I was speaking to you directly, sharing with you my beliefs about what is important when it comes to changing our lives and realising success.

Part 2 will examine factors which affect our lives and influence our ability to change. Certain themes will recur throughout to reinforce deeply the principles in your subconscious mind. Like a reference section, it is written to be dipped into or read in sequence, whichever you find most useful.

Part 3 is a series of simple but effective visualisation exercises which will put into practice the knowledge you have learnt.

Don't rush through each chapter, take your time to read, and comprehend the information and guidance in each chapter.

But First A Tale

A man sat at a table in a large restaurant, staring absentmindedly at nothing in particular, in a daydream. The waiter approached him and asked if everything was all right. Startled, the diner looked up and noticed that the waiter was in fact God. He stared at him for a moment and then looked down at the table. 'No' he said bitterly, 'No, everything is not all right. You see, this is not the life I ordered – I ordered something better, something full of joy and success. I wanted money, lots and lots of money, and, oh, by the way, I wanted to be thin. And while you're asking you may as well take note, pal, that I wanted to find true love, a nice car, women to find me attractive, plus I really wanted to speak a couple of languages, to master foreign cuisine and to see the world. So since you're asking everything is not alright, this is not the life I ordered, I wanted something better. Not this.'

Still staring at the table the diner heard God speak in a calm and easy voice.

'Well, change it. You know – you can change your life any day you want to.'

Then the diner looked up and God was gone. As he looked around the restaurant all he could see were the other diners staring up into the space where their waiters had stood.

PART 1

THINGS YOU NEED TO CONSIDER

CHAPTER 1

JUST...THINK!

The single greatest tool you have for changing your life, creating personal success, being happy, and living the life you wish, is within you. This tool is the power of active thought.

Your ability to think is the key to changing your life. Your mind is the most advanced organic matter in the known universe, more powerful that any computer in existence. It never stops working, it has spent 240 million years in nature's research and development laboratory. It is the source of all your emotions, beliefs and abilities. It is at your disposal – how you use it is up to you.

And yet it seems not only that most people fail to utilise this phenomenal resource, but that they do not know how to use it because they never realised they could.

Your mind is capable of solving every challenge you encounter; it is at your command. However, it is exactly like a computer in that it needs instruction before it can take action – albeit a phenomenally sophisticated and priceless computer that is capable of achieving more than you could ever believe possible.

Your ability to change your life will be found in your ability to harness and master the power of thought – the power that is in your brain. Just as a computer needs software to operate far beyond its basic internal operating system, so we too need software to operate at our highest level far beyond our basic internal responses such as breathing, blinking and so on. The big difference is that unlike computers, which rely on someone else creating the software for them, we can create the personal software for ourselves. That is the power of conscious thought.

A man who does not think for himself, does not think at all.

Oscar Wilde (1854–1900)

WHAT IS THOUGHT?

That is a tough one. From the mystics to the neuro-physiologists there are many ideas about what exactly a thought is. So let me be clear about something: I do not know. I have read many books and essays on the subject, and if I had a definitive answer I would be delighted to share it with you. Sadly, I do not, so I cannot. In reality it is not important. It is far more important that you understand that your thoughts will have a massive impact on your life and that you really do have the power to create your personal success.

Many writers on success and personal development talk about the power of the mind. They range from esoteric mystics to those proponents of self-hypnosis. Their language and perspective vary greatly. But they are all talking about the same thing – harnessing the power of the mind to transform our lives.

> Our personal power is found in the force of our thoughts – it is our real strength

When we are exposed to the same thing again and again, when all the books we read repeat the same concepts, it is all too easy to get a feeling of 'I've heard this stuff before.' That is one of the major challenges we face, because as we hear the same thing over and over, it becomes tired and clichéd in our minds, and we stop hearing the truth contained within. But the truth is: change the way you think and you can change the way you live.

It doesn't matter that you've read it before. It is better to have one book whose knowledge you understand and apply, than a thousand books whose knowledge you only know and recite.

Do you want the next ten years of your life to be exactly the same as the last ten years? Or do you want them to be better, more fulfilling, with more professional success, more love, travel, moments of joy, simple happiness, feelings of fulfilment, money, laughter, well-being and fun. Take note that if you do nothing then the next ten years will be exactly the same as the last ten, because nothing changes until you change, and you cannot change until you change the way you think.

All that a man achieves and all that he fails to achieve is the direct result of his own thoughts.

James Allen (1864–1912)

We take our minds for granted. We accept the opinions and the beliefs that lie at the root of how we think. We assume little control over who and how we are. We imagine that is just the way it is. It isn't. Your current pattern of thought is responsible for how you feel about yourself and where you are in your life – the good news is you can change it if you want to.

YOU ARE IN CONTROL

Your thoughts and your will-power reside in your mind and, if you are an average person with average brain function, that means you have 100% control over both of them.

I imagine you are asking exactly what is this mysterious invisible force I have never seen that people call will-power? Does it really exist? Do I have any?

OK: let's deal with this conclusively, so as you read other sections of this book you will not have to question whether they are applicable to you. I want you to realise they are – and to do so I have a little exercise for you.

Lift your right hand and touch the top of your head with it very, very gently. Now that you have done this, I want you to answer one very important and life-changing question.

How did you make your right hand touch the top of your head?

Think about it for a moment: how did you make your arm and hand do exactly what you wanted it to do?

How?

You will probably think, 'Well I just did! I thought it and the arm followed the instruction'.

The movement can rightly be seen as the consequence of an act of thought or personal will-power . If you are a neurophysiologist you might think in terms of synaptic pathways and biochemical neurotransmitters. But what triggered them – what started the process? Whatever you believe is not as important as realising and remembering that you made it happen. It wasn't a reflex like a foot rising when the knee is knocked. By thinking, and unconsciously sending an instruction to the part of your brain that looks after the motor functions related to movement, you made it happen.

Is it really such a leap of faith to imagine that the same thought, the same will-power that enabled you to raise your arm could also enable you to change your life?

> It is wrong to believe that you do not have will-power – we
> all have will-power. However your ability positively to
> engage it is what will accelerate your progress

We are the sum total of our thoughts, yet many of them are so ingrained that we follow them without any awareness.

When you drive to work, get dressed in the morning or pick your nose in the car at the traffic lights, you are not doing it consciously although you are doing it automatically. You do not know you are doing it. How often have you driven to work without having any clear idea or memory of the journey? The same can be said of getting dressed in the morning or, I am sorry to say, picking your nose. If you don't believe me just watch drivers in cars stopped at traffic lights, and note how many have a finger hovering in the region of their nose completely unaware that others can see.

The revelation of thought takes men out of servitude into freedom

Ralph Waldo Emerson (1803–1882)

There are some people who are always late. When you ask them why, they say, 'I can't help it' or 'It's not my fault', or – my favourite – 'I come from a family of bad timekeepers'. They tell you as though it is an ancient family tradition that they are keen to uphold. In reality they are late because they 'think late'. I don't mean they are thinking about punctuality at a conscious level. Rather they have come to accept that they are late so often that they no longer challenge themselves about it, and just assume it's part of who they are.

> Either you shape your thoughts or your thoughts shape you

You can choose to take control of your life, and in the process create the right kind of thinking and apply will-power; or you can do nothing. If you choose to do nothing then nothing will change. The next phase of your life will be exactly the same as the last. You will carry on comfortably making claims of being unlucky, of being destined to be poor, late, unhappy – or whatever else you choose to believe you are.

All actions find their origins in thought

The more powerfully held and committed the thought, the more powerful the action that follows it. Do not underestimate the power of thought. It is essential that your thoughts are positive and focused on success, and that you become the master of your will. Do not for a moment believe that the changes you seek to make cannot be realised because some things are 'just the way they are'. They aren't. Change your thoughts and apply the power of your will.

You can change your life any moment you want to, but there is a condition – success in life is not found in how we work, but in the way that we think

Today's action becomes tomorrow's habit.

Anon

'Why do winners win?' It's an age-old question. I have read about, spoken to and learnt from anyone I felt could help me find the answer to this question. When I put my findings to the test I see that in the lives of many historical characters, inventors, explorers, breakthrough academics and record-breaking athletes, some common timeless features emerge. Whatever they achieved had existed in their mind long before they accomplished and experienced it for real. They had thought consciously about the goal they were seeking to realise; it took shape in their imaginations, they pursued that image with an unbending will to succeed, and they took action steps to make it happen.

This whole process might be summed up, as 'We become what we think about'. Or we become what we consciously dream about when we have willed our thoughts to convert dreams into action.

> Happiness is a state of mind

Just Do It

Whenever I used to buy any electronic device I would rush home and switch it on as soon as possible. Perhaps, if it looked a bit complicated, I might skim through the manual – and try my best to figure out how to operate it. Then when I had a technical problem I would call a friend of mine who was always able to tell me what to do. It was after my fourth call one day that he told me in exasperation and very firmly 'To R T D M'. When I asked him what he meant he was kind enough to translate the acronym for me: read the damn manual.

No matter how well intentioned our actions they will be wasted if we don't do the right things at the right time. To get the most out of this book I would encourage you to do the exercises. Don't think that they do not apply to you because you get it intellectually. Think again, and remember that knowledge alone is not power. Applied knowledge is power.

So break the habit of a lifetime and take positive action.

Our self-image and our habits tend to go together. Change one and you will automatically change the other.

Maxwell Maltz (1899–1974)

I would like you to do the following exercise (unless you're driving a car or operating heavy machinery in which case you shouldn't be reading this book either).

Exercise
10 Years From Today

SIT DOWN RELAX GET COMFORTABLE, AND DON'T FALL ASLEEP!

I want you to imagine it is ten years from today. You are standing in front of the mirror in your bathroom; you look ten years older (at least). You are bleary eyed and just waking up. You notice that you have put on some weight as you are getting ready to go to work. You are not living in the house of your dreams, but it is the best you can afford.

You are still working in the same business or industry; you have moved up into management but have been passed over for the really big jobs you wanted, and younger people are overtaking you. You haven't even had a decent vacation – in short, you're not living the life you had wished for. Time has run out and the realisation has come upon you that, unless you win the lottery, or are granted three wishes by a magic fairy you happen upon while taking a short cut home through the enchanted forest one night, this is about as good as it gets. It is all downhill from here.

Keep looking in the mirror.

Your relationship with your partner is OK. Your kids don't relate to you, they don't seem to hold you in the esteem you would like.

Your dream car is, well, just that: a dream. The money wasn't there for it. The dog has fleas, and your pants are too tight.

Now how do you feel? I mean really feel: what emotions are going through your body? I hope they are not too uncomfortable or distressing because that is not the intention of the exercise. I want to you to see a vivid portrait of your future ten years from now, and just imagine how you would feel.

Now imagine, if the little fairy you met in the enchanted forest said she could not grant you three wishes, but instead could take you back in time and leave you there for the sole purpose of giving you a second chance. But only up to a maximum of ten years.

Would you take the opportunity to go back and take a second chance?

How long would you take?

Well I want you to take the full ten years, because that brings you back to right here, right now.

All right, that is the exercise completed.

Do not wait; the time will never be 'just right.' Start where you stand, and work with whatever tools you may have at your command, and better tools will be found as you go along.

Napoleon Hill (1883–1970)

How often do we think: if I'd only known then what I know now, how different my life could have been? Today, now is a moment when you can write your future so that in ten years hence you have created your joy, your success, your happiness.

Your life is not predetermined or prefabricated. You are its architect and its builder. Do not get into the blame game whereby you see your misfortunes as being due to others. Yes, there are many jerks in the world; bullies, greedy people, selfish hypocrites and mean-spirited individuals who will delight in your misfortune. The profound truth I understand is best expressed by Eleanor Roosevelt who said, 'No one can make you feel inferior without your consent'. It is not other people who make you feel bad, it is you who allows yourself to feel bad.

From now on I want you to deny that permission to others, who in the past have made you feel like a failure, a loser or any other negative emotion you have experienced.

Whatever they said to you, remember, is just their opinion, it is not a scientific fact.

What you believe about yourself will have much more impact on you than other peoples' opinions.

> When you change your thinking you really can change your life

Today you can, if you want to, change your life and put yourself on the path to creating the future you want. To do it you will need to leave behind your prejudices, your cynicism, your disbelief, and any other useless baggage you do not need. You will have no use for it on this journey.

Earl Nightingale wrote a book called *The Strangest Secret*. He looked at why some people were successful and others not. He knew it was not education, environment or conditioning. He believed the power lay within our minds. He said that we move in the direction of our dominant thought. If your dominant thought is failure then you create failure. If your dominant thought is success you will create success.

REMEMBER

- Your thoughts are the source of your feelings, emotions, actions and successes
- Your ability to creatively think, is a powerful tool. Use it
- You are in control of the way you think, accept the responsibility

CHAPTER 2

THE STARTING POINT

Before we can go anywhere we need to know where we are starting from, otherwise it will be impossible to know in which direction to go.

I believe that many people feel unable to change simply because they do not really believe they can. They are not living the life they had imagined but they accept lives of comfortable familiarity. Where they are in reality and where they really wish to be are far apart. The gap can cause frustration, conflict – or just plain inertia.

The starting point is ourselves. Many people will tell you that they seek fulfilment and happiness, yet they look for it in the wrong place – in the accumulation of things or the approval of others. But I believe that happiness is found within ourselves, in our fulfilment of our goals and aspirations. It is our beginning and our end.

> Don't focus on what you cannot do, concentrate on what you can do, and then learn to do the things you cannot

True success is not a place, or an amount of money. There are many unhappy people who have it all, beautiful homes and wealth, but are very dissatisfied with their life. Real success is a feeling, found when we learn to love ourselves unconditionally. With that love comes confidence, self-respect and the understanding that each and every one of us is unique. We learn that comparing ourselves to anyone else is a pointless exercise. Our happiness is found in realising our free will, in understanding that we can change our life any time we choose to and that we can make a difference to our own lives and the lives of the people we come into contact with each day.

In today's world we are overwhelmed with information. We have so much to do and so much stuff in our lives that it can be paralysing. We get busy, never have enough time to fit everything in and all it gives us is stress. In many ways we are so governed by time that we spend our days planning future dates, appointments and events we need to deal with and the only happy times we can remember are the good old days.

The past is gone. The future does not exist. We create the future in the here and now. Make a conscious effort to be where you are and give your full attention to the present. In so doing you will take the right actions to create the future you want

WHAT TIME IS IT?

If you asked a wolf in the wild, 'What time is it?' – assuming Dr Dolittle was there to act as an interpreter – so the animal knew exactly what you were saying – the wolf, having no knowledge of time, would (I imagine) answer, 'It's now.'

Yet if we were able to teach the wolf the concept of time and how to measure accurately the passage of time, would it benefit the animal?

I imagine a child of two or three might answer in the same way as the wolf. To a child there is 'now'. Children have no concept of time: they live in the present. Similarly if you ask a child of three or four 'Are you happy?' they will almost certainly say, 'Yes', unless they have just had an upset over some incident, which is soon forgotten.

Happiness is not time dependent. It doesn't await us at a point in the future. It is found in the present moment.

As we grow up, many childhood ambitions get left behind because, somewhere along the way, we stop believing in ourselves and grow instead fearful of failure or ridicule. We become like the wolf taught to tell the time – diverted from what is really important, which is being happy and believing that we can be successful at whatever we choose.

As the years pass we absorb more and more information that diverts away from what we want to do in life rather than helping us. The things that truly engage us we now seek to avoid. Fears and worries distract us. Our dreams become distant memories, our attention goes from being happy in the here and now, to 'things' in our future that we must avoid. It happens to us all. Day-to-day life gets in the way, responsibilities take over, there is no longer someone to pick us up when we fall over.

Our dreams die, and we lose our way. Now we need to find out where we are.

Have you ever been lost in a strange city with no idea which way to go, no one to ask, and no street map? You take your best guess as to where you think you might be, and you start walking?

You do not know if you are headed in the right direction, so you put hope above knowledge. I am all for hope. Sometimes in the darkest moments of our lives hope is all we have. It keeps us alive, but it is not a navigational aid.

You find a public telephone, and you phone a friend. 'Hey, I'm lost,' you say in mild frustration (this changes depending on the time of day and how tired you are). What does your friend say?

'Where are you?' Or if they are not prone to stating the obvious, they might ask you, 'What can you see?'

Before we can begin to change we need to know where we are in our life.

All journeys begin in our head, because we 'see' the destination and the journey in our mind. We imagine it. The route we take is always created in our heads. Then through conscious choice we either take action, or (as is more often the case) we do nothing at all.

KNOW YOURSELF: WHAT ARE YOUR STRENGTHS AND WHAT ARE YOUR WEAKNESSES?

It is strange how we often ignore or belittle our good qualities. I talk to many people who are looking to change and when I ask them what they are good and bad at, the list of negatives is always a lot longer than the positives. People focus on the negative because their expectations are low so they expect the worst and hope for the best.

Know yourself, master yourself.
Conquest of self is most gratifying

Unknown

And because they are concentrating on their weaknesses they rarely see their strengths as the wonderful assets they are because they are focusing so hard on the negative.

You cannot change your life if you are working from the familiar blueprint of your old self-image. The first thing you have to change is your expectation, and the way to do that is not to dwell on your weaknesses, but to concentrate on your strengths.

LIVING ON AUTOPILOT

We often do things without really thinking, which is very useful when it comes to repetitive everyday actions like walking, brushing teeth or answering the phone. In fact not only is it useful, it is fantastic – another example of the brain's ability to work for us without conscious effort.

There are many more complex examples of us being on autopilot, such as driving between two places (home and work) where we will have no memory of the drive and we take the route without conscious thought, yet are completely alert (usually) to any dangers.

It is not such a long hop to understand that we also have the habit of failure so ingrained into our subconscious minds that these habits are regularly triggered without our being aware of it. It is only after close examination that we will be able identify our personal failure habits.

Once we have identified them we can replace them with their opposite: success mechanisms. Think of it like changing (or up-grading) computer software. Change the programme and you change the results.

> A habit cannot be broken, by wishing it away. You have to take action

Habit is defined as a pattern of behaviour acquired through frequent repetition. You are not born with habits but acquire them from the world around you, through repetition. As you were repeating certain actions, you did not consider whether they were good or bad for you in the long run, you just did them. There is an old saying: 'Monkey see, monkey do'. As you grow up, you copy those around you. Imitation is one of the primary ways we learn. Once you have developed these habits they become so deeply ingrained in your mind that you do not even know you are doing them.

We first make our habits, and then our habits make us.

John Dryden (1631–1700)

A military instructor once told me that recruits are made to repeat an action 1600 times before it becomes an automatic reflex.

A habit is simply a pattern of behaviour repeated until it becomes reflex and automatic. If nothing else I want this book to convince you that it is the power of thought that has the ability to change your world. When you successfully change one habit you will really believe that you can successfully change another and another.

Good habits are formed; bad habits we fall into.

Unknown

It is estimated that 99% of the behaviours we manifest in life are based on subconscious thought. Past experience and programming has gone into our deep subconscious memory. We need instead consciously to think, and then to act. Do not do it the other way round. Too often people act and then think, 'what happened?'

Think, then act. Step by step, hour by hour, action by action, make the habit change happen – break the bad habits once and for all.

We are what we repeatedly do. Excellence, then, is not an act, but a habit.

Aristotle (384–322 BC)

You probably know people who are always late. Whenever you arrange to meet them you just know they won't be there on time, they will apologise quickly and without much sincerity. For as long as you have known them they are always behind and their home is a bombsite. Yet at work they are noted for their punctuality, and their office is neat and orderly.

My belief is that it is a case of priorities. A job is important. To be promoted within the company you need to have a good work record etc. So you can rationalise why you need to work and the downside if you lost the job. It's easy to prioritise the work habit to the level of 'really important'.

But in your personal life you just don't care so much because – guess what? Friends are forgiving. It's just not that important.

I have a good friend called Dave. Twenty-five years ago Dave and I both worked downtown. He was in a big international bank, doing trades and selling bonds, and I worked in the mail room of an advertising agency – I just ended up working there by accident, as happens to many of us. I got one hour for lunch. We would arrange to meet at 1pm once a week for lunch together and to compare notes on our weekend adventures.

I was always there by 12.59. I have always been punctual as the idea of keeping someone waiting is plain rude to me. I will do my very best never to be late. Dave would appear at 1.10, tell me to stop moaning, and off we would go for our sandwich. One day I pressed my point as to why was he always late. He told me he figured that if he was late it was unlikely that he would be kept waiting himself. That was the reality, not the important phone calls that came through just before he was due to leave.

I told him that in future I would only ever wait five minutes and then leave. Which is exactly what I did the following week; he called me and was very annoyed. That was 25 years ago, Dave has never once been late for a meeting with me ever since. I know he still misses appointments and flights and may be late for other people, but not me.

Because, somewhere in his deep subconscious mind, my friend-
ship and the day I left him standing at St Paul's underground station
have made him reprogramme his punctuality habit when he meets
me.

REMEMBER

- Focus on your strengths, not your weaknesses
- Nothing will change until you take action
- Let go of the past, it is gone you cannot change it

CHAPTER 3

WHO DO YOU THINK YOU ARE?

Who do you think you are? This is a very important question because your ability to change will depend upon it. If you believe that you are stupid or unlucky or incapable of breaking lifelong habits then guess what – you will be 100% right. You hold your self-image deep in your subconscious. This image is the one that your mind uses as a reference point in finding your identity.

> If you truly believe you are a failure, your mind will do all it can both to create failure and also to interpret events in a way that supports your belief

Have you ever heard someone say about somebody else, 'Just who do they think they are?' It is a derogatory rhetorical question asked about someone they don't like, perhaps because they believe the person in question has got a big ego or an inflated sense of importance. It is not a good question, because you do not know – though you may make assumptions based on the information you have – the reality of the person's journey through life, the challenges they face, or the sadness they may live with.

However, it is a very good question to ask yourself. It might be easier if you rephrase the question as 'what do you believe to be true about yourself?' Many people grow up with thoughts and beliefs about themselves that are probably not based on fact; rather they are based on ill-informed comments, or dubious opinion. How many youngsters are told by their parents or carers that they are stupid, clumsy, unlovable, incapable of getting a good job, a disappointment, or a score of other comments, spoken out in anger or frustration. The child is forming his or her self-image all the time. Such comments casually made, and I am sure never intentioned to damage, can go a long way to forming a person's concept of who they think they are. By contrast, if the child gets continuous positive affirmations – that they are clever, capable, pretty, brave, strong then he or she will form an image congruent with that feedback.

In early childhood the feedback and reinforced messages we get, shape our sense of who we are: our self-image.

> What you believe about yourself to be true will influence how you see yourself, perceive others and interpret events. A negative belief will manifest negative experience as surely as a positive belief will manifest positive experience

So when you ask yourself, 'What do I believe to be true about myself?' the answers you come up with will include some objective, obviously true facts such as your height, your age, the colour of your eyes, that you cannot change. However, those other 'truths' that are based upon assumption, or other people's notions, must be examined closely. It is likely that many of the things you believe about yourself are not objectively true and that there is little if any supporting evidence for them other than your opinion.

So if you believe you are clumsy you will remember every clumsy moment, and think, 'Yup I'm clumsy'. This is because you will look for evidence that validates the deeply-held false image, rather than remember moments when you did something perfectly.

Permanence, perseverance and persistence in spite of all obstacles, discouragements, and impossibilities: it is this, that in all things distinguishes the strong soul from the weak.

Thomas Carlyle (1795–1881)

We remember things emotionally. This means that when you spill a drink or drop a plate it will have a stronger emotional association than when you do something perfectly. In fact you will hardly remember the moments of perfect co-ordination, because they are not part of 'who you think you are'. But that is something you can change if you determine to do so. Change your self-image and your belief will follow, so instead of looking for evidence that you are clumsy you will look for evidence that you are co-ordinated.

What you believe to be true becomes your reality. Remember until we can change our belief it will be impossible to change our reality

HAVE A GO

Here is a tip for creating success in your life. Do something.

You will discover that once you do something, something happens. It may not be what you want to happen but change will begin to occur, and the outcome of this change will either be to take you closer to or further away from your desired goal.

Do nothing and there is only one possible outcome: that is, something will happen over which you had no control and that you will probably interpret as fate, bad luck, or simply further evidence that nothing good ever happens to you.

Most people do nothing. They wait for something to happen, and don't worry about the responsibility of whether it's what they wanted. They are in an inactive state that causes them to spend their time being reactive to events over which they have no control. If you want to change your life it is essential to be pro-active, take responsibility, take action and make things happen.

Do not spend your time believing in some fatalist philosophy, which expresses itself in such thoughts as, 'Well, I'm not lucky, things never work out for me'. If that is your wholly created and owned belief then it will come to pass. The patterns of a lifetime re-emerge and fit into your narrow view of your world, where the evidence that you are not destined to be successful is once again witnessed, examined and re-inforced.

Knowing is not enough; we must apply. Willing is not enough; we must do.

Johann Wolfgang Von Goethe (1749–1832)

In the many lessons that life has taught me, one of the most important and effective is this: you make things happen by taking action. Until you take action you are living in a dream state where you spend all your time fantasising, perhaps believing that the universe will give you what you want if you visualise it long, hard and powerfully enough, repeat powerful mantras and affirmations, or read books like this. Well dreaming is only part of the equation: the other is that you must take action.

> Success will follow your last failure; we just do not know when that will be

When I was nineteen, I went hitchhiking through Europe one summer. I had hardly any money and what little I had was for food; generally I slept in fields or on beaches. It was an adventure. Towards the end I went to Cannes in the south of France, a popular destination with young travellers. I wandered around, took in the sights and as the money ran out, decided it was time to go home. Up very early the next morning I walked up and up a never-ending road that led to the entrance to the motorway. It took me over two hours, and when I arrived I saw about twenty-five other hitchhikers all trying to get a lift. I had never seen so many people at one place; and it could only mean one of two things. Either I had stumbled upon a hitchhikers' convention or – which I realised was the real reason – it was a hitchhikers' graveyard. The protocol was to walk to the back of the queue, the logic being that the person at the front would get into the first car that stopped, so that slowly but surely you would eventually work your way to the front. Which in my case it looked very much like I'd get there sometime in late autumn.

There was a large petrol station close by, and as I stood with the prospect of a very long and dull wait ahead, the sky darkened, the wind picked up and the temperature dropped rapidly. It was going to rain – big time.

I noticed a black Mini Cooper arrive and a beautiful girl got out to fill her tank. Reflecting upon my life at that exact moment, I rather wished I had a black Mini Cooper and a beautiful travelling companion, instead of looking like a refugee from a jumble sale.

Then an almighty clap of thunder shook the air and the rain began falling in biblical proportions. At once, without any rehearsal and as though choreographed by Busby Berkeley himself, every hitchhiker turned and ran for shelter in the petrol station. No sooner had we reached shelter than the ferocity of the rain and wind picked up; the full storm had arrived, the rain exploding into a fine mist. As I looked at the spot where I had only moments before stood pondering my life, I was struck by the thought – my Eureka moment – 'There's nobody there.'

I realised suddenly that I could go out and be the only person looking for a lift, even if only for a short moment, in the number one position. Though I would also be soaked to the skin in seconds I did not give it a second thought. I walked into the downpour, placed my rucksack at my feet and stuck out my thumb.

After a few minutes the black Mini Cooper raced by towards the motorway. I held out my thumb, smiling stoically as the car disappeared past me. I continued to stand, hoping my fellow hikers would admire my act of bravado and let me stay near the front of the queue, when the rain stopped. Then I heard a car horn honk. I looked up and saw the Mini Cooper about 100 yards away parked on the side of the road. I figured she had been waiting for the rain to ease off, when suddenly the car began reversing towards me. I watched it closely, along with twenty-four other hitchhikers, as it stopped about 10 yards away. Then the passenger door swung open and the beautiful girl leant over and said, 'Where are you going?'

I gave myself my best chance of success: 'I'm going home to Scotland'.

'Get in' she said.

I climbed in, dumped my pack in the back seat and apologised for being so wet. She said, 'You stood in the rain, you were very determined. I liked that'.

It turned out she was German and was going to visit her sister in Heidelberg; in fact she invited me to join her – but I really was going home.

I was desperate to get home. Five weeks on the road had left me tired and homesick. So I stood in the rain, and in the process got a lift in a wonderful car with a beautiful woman. I should have learnt a lesson that day . . . but I did not.

I spent the next ten years assuming that on that day I had just been lucky.

In life you always have two choices, do nothing or do something. Only when we do something do we give ourselves any real chance of success and accomplishment

REMEMBER

- How you think and feel about yourself, will be reflected in the way others think and feel about you
- Knowing is not and never has been enough, you have to take action (apply knowledge) to create change
- Until you change your belief, it will be impossible to change your reality

CHAPTER 4

DO YOUR BEST TO DO YOUR BEST

Give 100% of yourself to the task at hand. Do your best every time

A study on happiness identified six common features for fulfilment, one of the most revealing of which was that happy people have work or leisure activities that engage their skills. They enjoy what they do because it engages them.

Being engaged grounds us in the 'now' and enables us to maximise the experience of the moment. The whole situation we're in becomes positively enhanced. Have you ever been to a store to enquire about some product, or checked into a hotel after a very long journey, or maybe been seated at a dinner beside a stranger, and the person you are meeting for the very first time is clearly bored, uninterested and would rather not be there? He or she answers your questions functionally and you sense they'd rather you went away and stopped bothering them. They are not thinking about the task in hand; the chances are their minds are somewhere else.

The best efforts of a fine person is felt after we have left their presence.

Ralph Waldo Emerson (1803–1882)

You do not need a postgraduate medical degree from Vienna to conclude that these folks are not very happy with their current situation. The reason does not matter – but the outcome of meeting them does. They turn a chance encounter into a memorable experience for all the wrong reasons. They may not like their boss, have been made to work a double shift, or have just come out of a difficult relationship the day before. It doesn't matter. The fact that they are rude, distant or uninterested does – because they chose to be so. No one made them react to the situation as they did. They chose to treat the experience as boring, pointless and forgettable.

They could have chosen instead to take the opportunity to have a great moment with you, to have taken responsibility for giving you their full attention and doing their best to serve you well, not because it is their job, but because they want to do their best.

You will have met shop assistants who went out of their way to help. A hotel clerk who made you feel as though you were coming home, and strangers at a social event who made you feel as though you are one of the most interesting people in the world. We have all met people who are attentive, make the most of every situation, have a positive attitude. They too made a choice.

> Be happy, or sad, be in control or out of control. It's all a choice

Why are so many people unhappy with their work, their relationships and their lives? Is there a more demoralising comment than someone saying, 'What's the point?'

The point is, if you put nothing into your bank account then obviously you can take nothing out. If you put no time or effort into a relationship, then you too will get nothing out of it, and the same is true of life.

If we do not do our best, if our efforts are just going through the motions, if our hearts and souls are absent then we are not putting very much in. By contrast, when we really try we will feel differently, we will experience better self-esteem, and we will make a difference.

> Do your best to do your best every chance you get, with the reassurance that you could not have tried any harder or done any better

Muhammad Ali said that if he had been a street sweeper, he would have tried to be the best street sweeper in the world. He would have done his best to be the 'greatest', at whatever he applied himself to.

We can too.

REMEMBER

- Be 100 per cent focussed on your goals
- You choose your response to events, seek always to choose to be positive

CHAPTER 5

DON'T 'WANT'
– DETERMINE

Be passionate about your life. It is the only one you are going to have

How often do you find yourself beginning a sentence with the words 'I want'?

I want to be rich . . . be happy . . . travel . . . have more holidays . . . see more of my family . . . lose 20lbs . . . be successful. The list is endless.

The vast majority of people have a want list; it is natural enough. As children, when Christmas approached we were forever adding to the list of things we wanted Santa to bring us. As adults we still want things, 'I want to get fit' being one of the most popular demands we make of ourselves.

There is only one problem. As a child were you ever told the old adage, 'I want, I want . . . doesn't get'. We would be told that when we asked for something we either were not entitled to it, or did not deserve it. Without realising it our parents were teaching us one of the most valuable lessons in life; just wanting something does not get it for you. What does is determining to achieve it.

Our brains process the information we put into them, and act upon the instruction we give them. The subconscious mind then works towards realising the goals we have set. When you tell yourself that you want to get fit, the brain interprets the goal as *wanting* to get fit. Therefore as long as you are in a state of wanting the brain rightly believes that it has achieved the goal.

That is why you must give the brain the right instruction, such as 'I'm going to get fit by following a proper fitness programme'. This may sound somewhat laboured, and very few of us are used to talking to ourselves with such precision, but it works. It has been conclusively demonstrated that positive self-talk is effective in helping people achieve better results in their lives. The use of positive affirmations, such as 'I am getting fitter now' or 'I am moving towards success in my life' or 'I am brave and courageous and will face my fears in life with confidence', may all sound like bad dialogue from a 'B' movie – but they work. Forget about feeling silly using such language or thinking that it feels unnatural. In reality it sends a very clear and unambiguous message to your brain and as your success and ability to change your life depends on how you think and what you believe you should determine to do it and judge the results for yourself. You will be pleasantly surprised.

> Make your affirmations with a positive feeling of future success to enhance their effectiveness in your subconscious

Let me say it again loud and clear: you need to really believe in a thing for it to become real, so change your beliefs and you change your life.

KEEP ASSESSING THE SITUATION

Every day you should take a moment to review where you are in relation to where you want to be. Are you moving closer or further away?

We will all have heard a footballer who, when asked why he missed a goal, rolls out the time-tested cliché and state, with no sense of irony, that he took his eye off the ball. After a traffic accident a car driver will say he took his eye off the road for a moment. It is equally important in our journey through life that we keep our eyes clearly on the target, in the pursuit of our goals.

By keeping our eye on the target we can alter course, and still make sure we stay on track. The truly incredible thing is how often people lose sight of their life goals; they give up, or somehow get so distracted that they go way off track. You must continually assess where you are in relation to the life you want.

To change your life you need to acquire the new thoughts and beliefs that will enable you to change. The process will be immediate but the results will take time, which is why you will be able to see small incremental changes occur by keeping a clear picture of your progress.

We improve ourselves by victories over ourselves

Edward Gibbon (1737–1794)

Do not merely assume you are on track and making progress, get the proof to substantiate it. Get clear physical evidence that you are making progress: do not rely on feedback from close friends and loved ones. With the best will in the world they will hate to disappoint you, so they will always seek to give you positive news. Trust your own eyes only.

> We need constantly and honestly to appraise where we are in relation to our goals

In life when we get lost, it is easy to go into denial. We can and will convince ourselves that everything is OK, when everything is anything but that. We refuse offers of help for a variety of reasons: because we are too proud and because we do not want others to know that we are not the perfect people we imagine they think we are (chances are they don't). It is all too possible for self-delusion to ignore difficulties until the problem we denied overwhelms us.

If you are honest with yourself and deal with the situation you are in as it is, then you can take the appropriate action to resolve it – it may be slow, and painful – but you can do it. But if you are deluding yourself you will have the wrong idea of where you are. Based on the wrong information, every decision you make will be wrong too.

Every day, assess the situation; are you closer or further away from your goal? Are the changes you seek in life occurring? The answer to these questions will allow you to make a more informed choice. The steps that take you away from your goals must be identified and corrected. The progress you make will build a stronger and more positive self-image.

REMEMBER

- Don't be vague or half-hearted, in defining your goals
- Be honest with yourself, otherwise the only person you are fooling is yourself

CHAPTER 6

GET A PLAN – THEN MAKE IT HAPPEN!

Having a plan is as old as time itself. I am sure that cavemen had one when they went hunting. No goal that you seek just happens, it must be planned, and the plan must be broken down into a series of smaller more manageable goals, which act as markers of progress.

A friend of mine has had a rags-to-riches life. After finishing education early, he set out with a burning ambition to be successful. He saw his future in sales. Forty years later his company is listed on the stock market with offices in the US and UK. It is worth over $200 million and he is a very wealthy man, still involved in the business he created, his time spent planning, thinking through the steps that need to be taken to realise the big goals he has set for the company. I spent a day with him at his home where he has lived for over twenty years and we talked about the lessons he had learnt in life. He had experienced many highs and lows. He had stared defeat and ruin in the face many times. He had lived a real life with all its twists and turns. In the past few years he had also overcome cancer and been through major surgery on two occasions.

I asked him what advice he would give someone in the pursuit of their goal, either personal or professional. He thought for a moment and said, 'You make it happen!'

Achieving the ultimate goal will occur as the result of a series of small goals. Without planning the steps you need to take, you will waste a lot of time and energy going round in circles and not moving forward. You will fritter away the most precious commodity you have – time.

One final thought. If your plan isn't working, then change it – it is allowed.

> You have to make things happen, because your goal is not going simply to achieve itself. You have to plan it, and then take action to make it happen

WHAT ARE YOU WAITING FOR? TAKE THE FIRST STEP

You must take that first step. Do not falter, do not hesitate. You are going from the known to the unknown, but only for an instant. As soon as you step forward, you will have put into motion the process of change. You will never be the same person again – because you have taken action, yet for so many people taking that first step is just too hard, so they never do it.

Things do not change; we change.

Henry David Thoreau (1817–1862)

The reason it is hard to take the first step is because we have to abandon our natural fear of failure. It is like letting go of the side of the swimming pool and taking the first scary stroke in deep water, fearing we may sink, and finding we can swim. Or when we ride our bike without stabilisers for the first time and suddenly our father or mother lets go – and we keep going. Suddenly we discover that we are capable of so much more than what we had until that instant believed. But we had to let go and take the first step to make that discovery.

I have learnt through my friends and clients that if people do not want to change then they will not change. You cannot make them change if they do not want to.

The only person in the world you can change is yourself, and it begins with a small step, then another. I want it to inspire you to believe you really can change your life, and then – do so.

REMEMBER

- If you fail to plan then you are planning to fail
- Desire and motivation without planning and action, is just daydreaming

PART 2

THINGS YOU NEED TO KNOW

CHAPTER 1

BELIEFS

What do you believe about yourself?

Do you believe you are clever, attractive, capable and lucky? Or are you stupid, clumsy, inept and unlucky?

I believe that what you believe about yourself shapes the way you perceive the world and, how the world perceives you.

When you believe you can achieve something, you give yourself every chance to do it. When you believe you cannot do something, it is almost a certainty that you will not do it. Confused? Let me explain this in more detail.

IS THE WORLD FLAT?

If you believe something to be true, then you will look for evidence that reinforces that belief. When you experience evidence to the contrary, you simply ignore it or refuse to accept it. Let's take an extreme example that at the time I found very funny.

Twenty-five years ago I was walking in London one Sunday afternoon and I came upon Speakers Corner in Hyde Park. It is a famous landmark because anybody can get up there and make a speech on any topic they want – it's the democratic ideal of freedom of speech. Every person has a voice and they are free to express their views and opinions secure in the knowledge that they will not be put in the back of a police wagon and taken somewhere never to be seen again. You get a cross-section of the world there including extremists, fanatics, and eccentrics. Sometimes people will have no audience at all or maybe just two or three people will be listening. Sometimes, when there is a politically or religiously charged speaker, there will be hundreds caught up in passionate debate. The one thing that the speakers have in common is their strong belief in their subject matter. So there I was wandering through when I came upon a fellow standing on a stepladder telling the world that he was a member of the Flat Earth Society. He made a strong and convincing argument that the earth was indeed flat. When asked by one of the four spectators, 'What about the photographs from space?' he did not hesitate. With absolute conviction he replied, 'They've been forged, part of a great conspiracy.'

I was astonished and didn't know if he was serious or not, but he continued earnestly to insist that the earth was flat, no matter what the objection.

Before we had scientific proof, people believed that the world was indeed flat. Ancient maps depicted it as such and the belief was that when you reached the edge of the earth, you simply sailed off, or fell off, into space. Now if you truly, powerfully believe the earth is flat, and are closed to accepting any other evidence, your belief, powerfully held, will protect you. It will protect you from hearing or accepting any contrary evidence; you are not open to it. So this fellow in the park was a perfect example – irrespective of conclusive scientific evidence, he believed what it suited him to believe.

> What you believe about yourself to be true will influence not just the way you feel about yourself. Critically, it will also influence the way the world sees you and how you perceive the world

How Do You See The World?

Children are born with no prejudices, no belief systems and no opinions. They have been equipped by nature to learn to survive as rapidly as possible. Just like sponges they absorb every piece of information they can. They depend upon their parents to survive, and use their power of reasoning to make sense of their world. What a child believes about itself and the world around it is not dependent on whether it was born into wealth or poverty, had one parent or two or on any other physical factors. It is about what it was taught to believe, and had reinforced as it developed.

The size of your success is determined by the size of your belief.

Anon

As we get older, more independent of a parent or peer group to shape our beliefs, we end up finding our own reinforcements for the taught beliefs of our early childhood. We have heard of the extremist children of parents who hold extreme religious, political and racial views, children who believe that they are ethnically superior to others. Their religion is the only religion, their way of living the only right way to live. The beliefs so powerfully imprinted on their minds as children influence them into adulthood in how they think, feel and act.

The good news is that we can choose to change our beliefs. But first we have to examine them – we have to put them under the microscope and examine their authenticity

Ask yourself whether your beliefs about yourself are based on truth and honest understanding, or are they based on past conditioning, falsehood and erroneous thinking? If we have an erroneous belief that we accept to be true and authentic, we will not question it. We are going to make decisions based on misinformation, and inevitably they will take us in the wrong direction.

What do you believe you cannot do? When somebody invites you to try something you believe you cannot do, what do you say? Is it, 'I can't'? If asked why, do you answer with the assertion that, 'I've tried and I just can't!'? The truth is that you won't because of your powerful belief in your inability to succeed. It is not because of your (imagined) lack of ability. Your expectation of failure was the reason, you said 'I can't' and the reason you have given up trying.

We are what we believe we are

Benjamin N. Cardozo U.S. Supreme Court Judge
(1870–1938)

There is a great irony in life. If we put wrong beliefs into our mind for whatever reason, they will act as a block to stop us achieving the things we so wish to achieve. Yet more often than not when you examine your beliefs about yourself, you will find that many of them are false. They were planted in our head by others, often in childhood. We have learnt and reinforced them because they made us feel safe or protected from failure. So challenge what you believe about yourself; ask where those beliefs came from, and determine to change them.

BELIEVE YOU CAN

When you study the lives of famous people who have achieved great things, you often discover a parent, relative, or teacher who gave them an unshakeable belief in their ability to succeed.

I came across a story of a young man who was brought up in a small town in America. His family were poor. They lived in a trailer. When he was three years old, his mother left home never to return. The father was a roofing contractor who did his best to bring up the boy on his own, but the pressure of life and poverty wore him down, and he became a hopeless alcoholic, every night returning home drunk. The son would take care of himself before going to bed. Eventually the father was deemed an unfit parent, the boy was taken into care and shortly thereafter his father died. The son went to college, started his own business and became a success in the community. In his early thirties, he was invited to become the mayor of the town. At the ceremony, homage was paid to his achievements. Afterwards a journalist said to him, how proud the city was of his achievements especially given the hard start that he had had in life with an alcoholic father who could not care for him. The young man looked at the journalist and said, 'You're wrong to assume that I am here today in spite of my father. My father was an alcoholic. He found life very hard, but every night when he came home, he would come to my room and apologise for being drunk and tell me that he loved me. He told me to believe that I could do anything that I put my mind to. He would apologise tearfully for being the way he was. He wanted me to know that I could be anything that I wanted to be. I'm here because of my father.'

His father's belief was powerfully planted in that young man and it shaped the way he saw himself and the world ahead of him. He was enabled by belief in himself.

It is wonderful when someone really believes in you. It is amazing how their belief in you actually strengthens your belief in yourself. But above all you must believe in yourself and you must challenge your beliefs to see if they are real or imagined. Your beliefs in themselves are neither good nor bad but their effect can be positive or negative. They shape the way you see the world and enable you to achieve the success you want, which is why you must examine them, and decide for yourself.

A positive belief in yourself is the most important belief of all

The beliefs that you have in your life will stay with you for life, unless you examine them or learn from an experience that brings them into question. If you believe that you are unlovable, inadequate or ugly, if you believe that you are stupid, incapable or incompetent, and you do not challenge that belief it will stay with you. You will unconsciously create within you a stop that will limit your future success. At some point, when your beliefs are challenged by the world – for example when you are offered a job that you just don't believe you are capable of, though other people can tell that you are – you will unconsciously sabotage yourself because the belief will not allow you to become a person in this new position. It is vital that you understand the impact your beliefs have on your life and the lives of those around you. They are latent: they exist without our being totally aware of them. And yet they shape our expectations. And our expectations influence our attitudes, which in turn influence our outcomes.

If you believe in something, no proof is necessary. If you don't none is sufficient.

Unknown

CHALLENGE YOURSELF

If you don't challenge your beliefs they limit and imprison you. I have met people who told me they were shy, that they had always been shy as children – that is how it was, and always would be. It is a great tragedy in life that our unfounded beliefs confine us, and that we accept them as given. We do not challenge them because we think they are true. When your mind believes something to be true, it will, at a subconscious level, perform the necessary actions to help you maintain that belief. When we take it upon ourselves to challenge a negative belief, we back away from it because we become afraid.

Live your beliefs and you can turn the world around.

Henry David Thoreau (1817–1862)

As we grow up we develop beliefs that shape the way we think and act. Some are true and some are false. Most people do not want to give up their beliefs because in them they find their sense of identity – or at least they think they do. In the introduction to this book I said that you can change your life, any day you want to, if you can change the way you think. Begin by considering your beliefs.

HOW EXPECTATIONS INFLUENCE PERCEPTION

There was a widowed farmer in ancient times. He had two sons who were three years apart in age. When the elder son got to the age of fifteen, the farmer, unable to offer him any work on the farm, walked with him to town in the hope that he would find work there or on a larger farm along the way. As he bid his son farewell, on his journey into life, he told him, 'Don't trust anybody son because everyone will try to steal from you. If you let them they will. Most people are selfish, so look after yourself: always put yourself first'.

The son tearfully hugged his father and with the advice given to him set out into the world. Three years later the younger boy came of age to leave home. In the time that had passed the father had fallen in love and married again. He had mellowed with age, he smiled a lot more, his life felt good, and walking his son to town this time he said, 'Son, go and see the world, find the joy that lies out there. And to your fellow man, trust them, love them, care for them, show compassion and it will be shown to you – what you give to the world, the world will give back to you with interest. Oh and one other thing, son: a life without love is a life half-lived. Find a woman that you can love, and allow her to love you, then you will have the world'. The brothers had no contact as their lives took them to different parts of the country. Many years later, the father died, and the sons returned for the funeral and they met for the first time in twenty-five years. They described their adventures since leaving home, and each had found the world to be exactly as his father described it.

Man is what he believes

Anton Chekhov (1860–1904)

BELIEFS AND INTELLIGENCE

Your beliefs are the blueprint in your life. Get them right and every-thing will follow; get them wrong and you will just be pushing against life itself. The power of belief cannot be underestimated, especially in the way that it can enable you to face the challenges of life and to persist through the hardships, finding a strong and powerful sense deep within yourself of being able to accomplish even the seemingly impossible.

It is important to note that intelligence is not the greatest indicator to our future success in life. Self-image and self-beliefs are the real indicators. For instance research shows that there is no correlation between academic success and earning ability. Your earning ability is related to the qualities of passion, desire, determination, commitment, and belief. These things are not learned academically. What you believe, visualise and think about most, you can turn into your reality. You can change your life by changing your belief.

> What you believe to be true, in your mind becomes true so you must question your beliefs and examine their authenticity

Look at the feats of sporting high achievement. How many false and limiting beliefs in sport have been held by physiologists and sports physicians, indeed by trainers themselves? We only have to think of the four-minute mile. Back in the Forties and the early Fifties it was believed physically impossible that a human being could run a mile in fewer than four minutes. Since that belief was shattered by one man who believed he could do it, it has been done many tens of thousands of times. Similarly it was once believed that no man could climb to the summit of Mount Everest because the human body could not cope with the altitude at 29,000ft and yet it has been done by many hundreds of people since. All it took was for someone to believe differently, and act on their belief.

> You must challenge the beliefs that you think hold you back. If you do not challenge them, they will stay with you to shape your destiny and your future will merely be a complete repetition of your past. If you want your life to develop in positive ways, if you want to achieve joy, fulfilment, happiness, love and all the best things that this world can offer, you first must look at what you believe

THE POWER OF BELIEF

And above all things, never think
that you're not good enough
yourself. A man should never think
that. My belief is that in life people
will take you at your own reckoning.

Anthony Trollope (1815–1882)

One of the fathers of the personal development movement was a man called Napoleon Hill. He wrote a classic best seller which is still in print today and still widely read called *Think, and Grow Rich*. He wrote the following words, 'Whatever the mind of men conceive and believe, it can achieve'. When I first read phrases like this, I scoffed at them; they just seemed too unscientific and fluffy, written to give hope to the hopeless. I now know they are true. Everything you do starts life as a thought in your mind. Powerfully held, visualised and believed in, it begins a life of its own. In fact what actually happens is that our brains focus intently on bringing that visualised concept, that visualised ideal, into our reality.

That is how we are able to spot opportunities, which some people call coincidence.

There is no such thing as coincidence

BELIEFS THAT INFLUENCE

What did the great leaders through history have in common? How did they get so many people to believe in them? In short what exactly is leadership? I think of it in terms of follower-ship. Leaders inspire people to follow them, by their strong sense of belief in themselves, their objectives, and their absolute ability to achieve them. They communicate that belief through their words and actions, and people have confidence in them – and are inspired by them. Confidence comes from having faith in yourself. When you meet a person who is truly confident, you sense it, they don't have to say anything, no one has to tell you, you just feel it. Their belief in themselves communicates itself.

If you think you can win, you can win. Faith is necessary to victory

William Hazlitt, English essayist (1778–1830)

What you believe about yourself is held deeply in your subconscious mind, and influences the way it interprets information. Expectations you believe in tend to be realised. Take a simple example; if you believe you are clumsy, your expectation is that you will drop more glasses or plates than the average person, that you will stub your toe more often, catch your thumb or bump your head – all because you think you are clumsy. In your subconscious mind this is the self-image you hold to be true. Your expectation is that things will happen that demonstrate your clumsiness. So when placing a glass on a table your subconscious mind may expect you to drop the glass without you being aware. That expectation inhibits concentration and an accident results, and this reinforces the belief you held. It is important that you take this on board. Your beliefs are going to shape everything that happens in your life.

> Believe in yourself. You were not born to fail. You do not
> need permission to be happy

LOOK WHERE YOU ARE GOING

Unfortunately in life most people focus on their most powerful beliefs which tend to be negative. They focus on their faults and continually review and remember them. They find fault in others too, and in the process they reinforce their prejudices. But their beliefs are unexamined. According to research, by the time we have reached the age of two, 50% of our belief system has been determined. By the age of eight years about 80% is in place, and by fifteen between 85–90% of the beliefs you hold to be true will, if they remain unchallenged, stay with you for the rest of your life. And yet most of our learning during this time was unconscious, we simply copied the behaviour of others we admired or feared, we sought the approval of our parents and we did the things that would get us love and praise.

The universe is change; our life is what our thoughts make it.

Marcus Aurelius Antoninus, Roman emperor (121–180 AD)

Others were shaping our self-image to begin with, then we took over. It might help to think of your belief system as software that has been coded into your mind allowing you to operate without any awareness; it shapes your self-image. I am saddened when I hear of teenagers who go through a terrible time of believing they are unattractive and that no one understands or cares about them. Lacking confidence, they develop a negative self-image, and construct their world around imagined truths rather than real facts. They have come to accept those false beliefs as true. Imagine the difference you could make to the lives of teenagers if you could just reinforce positive belief in them. Encourage them to think well of themselves, to believe they can succeed like the young man whose alcoholic father, dismissed by the world around him as an abject failure, gave his son the powerful belief that he was capable of being anything he put his mind to. The fact that 90% of your beliefs are in place by the age of fifteen does not mean that you cannot challenge them and completely change them.

> It's up to you to choose the direction of your life

You can change your beliefs in a moment, and change your life. But only you can do it. You begin by changing them to positive thoughts and expectations about yourself and your ability to succeed.

REMEMBER

- You can change your beliefs
- You are what you believe you are
- A positive belief in yourself and your ability to succeed is at the heart of your ability to change your life

CHAPTER 2

GOALS

Imagine you are introduced to the greatest archer in the world, a wise old chap from Japan who is a master of the bow and arrow. You ask him to demonstrate his skill to you, but the only place available is a big, wide, open empty field. So you take this master to the middle of the empty field and you say to him, 'OK, show me how good you are'. The master glances around and he looks at you and he says, 'Well, what do you want me to aim at?' There are no targets in the field; there is nothing for him to aim at, so irrespective of how brilliant and talented he is, it would be impossible for him to demonstrate his skill without a target to aim for. What does the master do? I suspect he would simply fire an arrow to a point in the field, and then – whilst you are on the point of saying that didn't seem so skillful – he would take a second arrow out and fire it directly down the shaft of the first and then proceed to put more arrows into the exact same spot. For once he had the first arrow in the ground, he had a target to aim for. Your brain needs targets to aim at; it is how we are conditioned. You may be familiar with the concept of having a goal, a target, a vision, and a dream. The most common term for having a personal target to aim at is called goal-setting. It is important in our lives that we have goals to aim for, and dreams that inspire us.

If you do not have a target to aim for – what are you going to hit?

Many people simply just have vague dreams and desires; they are no more than wishes that will probably never be fulfilled in their lives. But when you set a specific and clear target, a goal that you can visualise clearly, then like the archer after the first arrow in the ground you have a target to aim for. Your mind, your brilliant, fantastic, beautifully creative mind will lock onto this target and do everything in its power to bring to your attention everything that will help you realise your goal.

It is important that we have goals in our lives. These goals should be to do with our health, our hearts, our careers, our financial well being, our travels, because if we don't set goals we will end up where random chance blows us.

Many people want to be successful but they do not define what success looks like

IMAGINE YOU MET A GENIE

When we were children, we had stories read to us. The stories often related to fairies, wizards, and the ever popular magic genie in the bottle. These characters all had one thing in common: they could grant people wishes. Do you remember the fairy godmother granting three wishes in the storybooks that you read? As children we would say, 'If I had three wishes I would wish for . . .' and normally they were fanciful thoughts from our imaginations, chocolate mountains, lots of our favourite toys, very straight-forward things, because as a child our pleasures were simple. As we get older we stop wishing and we start hoping that we might win the lottery, but it's just as fanciful.

Man is a goal-seeking animal. His life only has meaning if he is reaching out and striving for his goals.

Aristotle (384–322 BC)

There was a man who after many years of poverty and hardship walks into the church, falls at the knees and looks at the altar and says, 'God, I've done my best to be a good man, I've worked hard, but I have nothing to show for my life, if only I could win the lottery, please help me.'

A week later, still with no luck, the man went back on his knees and this time he implored the Lord, 'Please Lord, I'm begging you, just once, help me win the lottery, help me from this wretched life of poverty that I may experience what wealth can give a man.'

And still nothing. However he was a stubborn man and deter-mined so, finally, he went back to the church, he dropped on his knees, he looked up once again, and with tears in his eyes said, 'Please, I'm begging you, just once. Reward this humble, holy man who has done his best to serve you well, all I ask of you is that you please, please, please let me win the lottery.'

At that exact moment there was a rumbling in the sky and a beam of light shone down into the church and a deep God-like voice said, 'OK, I will, but do me a favour go and buy a lottery ticket first . . . please.'

If you fail to set yourself a target, a clearly defined goal, you will more than likely end up wandering at random

NOTHING HAPPENS UNTIL WE TAKE ACTION

We cannot take action until we know exactly what it is that we want to achieve or we need to do. For many people this is quite simply the hardest part of their life journey: they don't know what they want. I have asked many young people what it is they want from life. They often reply by saying things like 'I don't want to be unhappy', 'I don't want to live alone', 'I don't want to worry about having no money', 'I don't want to live in a house that is small', 'I don't want to be lonely', 'I don't want to be sad'. And it strikes me that they know what they do not want and have clearly defined it in their mind – they don't want feelings of inadequacy or desperation or fear. But they have not defined what it is they want. Those people who go on to achieve success in their life – and I do not mean spectacular power or wealth, I mean a personal sense of achievement, know exactly what they want in life. Setting up their own small business, being financially independent, being in a loving relationship: whatever it is, they identified what it was they wanted in considerable detail, before they began taking the appropriate action to achieve it.

IT'S EASY TO WANDER AND GET LOST IF YOU LACK CLARITY

I have been to school reunions and met people who have spent twenty years doing the same thing year in and year out and then just shrugging their shoulders and saying 'well, that's life – what can you do about it'? The answer is you can do everything about it. In my previous book *Natural Born Winners* I paid a lot of attention to the importance of setting clear goals. There were certain golden rules I explained that had to be applied to setting of goals and they are as follows: first, you must clearly define your goal in precise visual, emotive terms. This means that when you describe your goal to another person they too can get a clear idea of exactly what it is you are trying to achieve. Thus you would not describe your goal as, 'I want to be better' or 'I want to be happier', you would define what 'better' looks like. You would say, I am going to lose 20lbs in weight, I am going to join a gym, I am going to start my own business with a small stall in the market place selling foreign pottery that I will import from South America. You will define exactly what it is you are going to do. The second thing you must do is get emotionally connected to the feelings that achieving the goal will bring you, so you define the goal in terms that give you a feeling of success. Now when you visualise the goal and you 'see' it in your mind, it becomes the target your subconscious mind aims for.

The third aspect is to create a dimension of time. You must set a date by which the goal will be achieved even if that date is months or years out.

What you get by achieving your goals is not as important as what you become by achieving your goals.

Johann Wolfgang von Goethe (1749–1832)

THE TWO MOST IMPORTANT QUESTIONS IN LIFE

I am sure that the two most important questions in life are: 'Where do you want to go?' and 'When do you want to get there?'

They are the two most important questions because once you know the where and the when, your subconscious mind will find the how.

That untapped resource, the subconscious, will find the solution for you. It will almost deliver it in front of you. Your first awareness will be that marvellous eureka moment. At first your reaction might be:

'What a coincidence' or 'How did that happen?' or 'That was magical'.

In reality you have trusted your subconscious mind to do what it does best – that is, focus through its beliefs on finding solutions to challenges. So you must remember where and when. Where do you want to go and when do you want to get there. The where is your goal, and the when is your date. You set the date, and as you go towards it you can measure your progress towards your goal and see if you are on schedule to achieving it.

> Show me a successful person, and I will show you a person who has set themselves clear goals

Few people have defined goals for their lives. They don't plan their future in anything like the detail they will plan a two-week holiday, or a Friday evening dinner party in their house. Why is this? I think that, when we dream of big achievements and the goals we would like to reach, our belief system drags us down. If our belief system is negative or has low expectations, it subconsciously convinces us that we cannot succeed. As previously mentioned we think in accordance with our belief system, and we tell ourselves, 'I couldn't be a professional singer.' 'I could never run a marathon.' 'I guess being your own boss is for other people, not me.' The failure mechanism, which has kept us back for so many years, kicks in and fires up with turbo-charged power to keep us there.

You must have big dreams for yourself: for your life, for your heart, for your hopes, for your health, for your wealth. The things in life that are going to give you feelings of worth, joy and happiness can only be achieved when we set the big goals and believe beyond any doubt that we can achieve them.

Never make the mistake of assuming that people who are successful have just been lucky

All our achievements in life are born in our imaginations. The beautiful buildings that you have admired throughout the world did not just happen: they existed as goals in the mind of the architect before they put pen to paper. The aircraft that takes you on vacation or flies at the speed of sound exists only because somebody somewhere had a goal to create it and set about making it happen.

THOUGHT IS THE STARTING POINT

The power of thought is the starting point; thought is the originator of all our ideas. It is the home of our imaginations, our emotions, our belief, our will-power. It follows as I said before, that you can change your life when you change the way you think. So right now what are your goals in life? When you are looking back as an elderly person sitting in the sunshine in Florida or wherever you want to be, what would you want to look back on with the greatest pride? What would it be: saving a life, making a positive difference, climbing a previously unclimbed mountain, raising a family to the very best of your ability, or just being plain happy?

Go confidently in the direction of your dreams. Live the life you have imagined.

Henry David Thoreau (1817–1862)

Make no mistake of the need to set clear goals. Defined goals are necessary to you achieving your success. The archer in the field could not demonstrate his skill without a target. He had to put the first arrow in the ground to create one. So it is for you: your goals can be massive, dramatic, spectacular, but you have to give them a clear definition; visualised and described; with a point in space and time; where and when. The biggest of your goals can always be defined in a series of smaller goals. Each one like a stepping stone, moving you closer and closer to your final destination.

> When you clearly define a goal, focus on it, visualise it, revisit it, believe in it, then you will move towards it. We create our own reality by our thoughts, beliefs and actions

MAKE IT A WORTHY GOAL

It goes without saying that the goals should be worthy goals; they should be goals that are good for you. Set yourself a goal that challenges and inspires you, that gets you excited about it, and you will refuse to let anything dampen your determination to succeed.

Or will you? You will have a great deal of enthusiasm when you begin, but with so many unrealised goals the enthusiasm fades. What is left behind is fatigue and disillusionment. When fatigue remains, we give up. It's the easiest thing we could ever do. That moment of giving up brings a momentary comfort that can be very soothing, but it will pass and the frustration will grow, and what we will have done is just reinforced a little more in our mind the belief that we simply cannot achieve the goals we set ourselves.

How can we avoid giving up? Many people go to the office in the morning, and they sit down and write their 'to do' list. Or at home many refrigerators have a magnetic notepad stuck to them on which is written a list of the items that need to be purchased from the store. These are goals in themselves. People write them down. Writing our goals down gives them clarity, and keeps us focused on what we need to accomplish. We think nothing of writing a shopping list or a to do list at work, yet we don't write a list down for our life. You can change that now. I said earlier, that when we set a goal, we must clearly define it. I am now asking you to write yours down. Writing it down makes it real – you have committed it to paper and you can revisit what you have written as often as you need to. Writing the goal down gives it strength and creates a memory of it in your mind that is more powerful than if you just gave it a passing thought.

> A goal without a plan is just a wish. A goal must have a plan, which you believe in and act upon, otherwise nothing will change. A goal on its own is never enough

Very few people sit down and take the time to ask themselves, 'What do I really want out of life'. Most of us just bumble through from day to day, struggling to get by, moaning about the job we have because it is not the job we want or because we feel unappreciated; complaining about the house we live in because it is not big enough; finding fault in our partners because they do not make us feel as good about ourselves as we think they should. We go through life asleep to the possibilities all around us.

Until you determine exactly what it is that you wish to achieve, it is impossible for you to achieve anything of any value. Goal setting is easy. But beware – no sooner will you have set the goal, than the negative beliefs will appear as a voice in the back of your mind saying, 'You'll never do it'. It requires dedication and determination to sit down, to spend time alone, thinking about the life you really want to live. Looking forward to that time way in the future when you can look back upon your life and think, 'Wow, I did all those things'.

I believe that there are two types of people in the world – those who talk, and those who do. Those who talk are never short of things to tell us, but those who do are the ones who inspire us by their actions. Are you a talker or are you a doer? Become someone who does the things that they set out to do.

A man without a goal is like a ship without a rudder.

Thomas Carlyle, Scottish essayist and historian
(1795–1881)

Fame, power and money are goals sought by many people, but they are illusory goals. They are not ends in themselves. These are illusions. What some hope to find in fame, power and money is the elusive quality in life we all seek: happiness, fulfilment and joy – real goals. So be careful in identifying what you are looking for.

Make a list of the goals you want to achieve in life, the experiences you want to have, the legacy you want to leave. Make a firm commitment to those goals, and believe that you can achieve them. Believe you can. Because when you believe you can, you will.

> Happiness is not found in things, it is found in ourselves. It is not a place, it is a state of mind, and when you believe you can achieve it, you will. But first you must define what happiness looks like for you

When you read interviews with people, particularly elderly people towards the ends of their lives, their regrets are not for the things at which they failed. The regrets are for the things they did not do. Only at the end of our days we recognise that all the things we have in life, our cars, our houses, money, youth, health, these things pass. What we keep are our memories and the contribution we made to the world.

A final word: many people set themselves goals and give up. Why? It happens so frequently and to so many people. The principle reason is fear: fear of failure, fear of rejection, fear of ridicule, fear of discovering we are inadequate, fear of discovering we are not the person we dreamed we could be. This fear is caused by our imaginations creating a worst case scenario, based on a belief that failure is inevitable – which is why we must change our beliefs. For only by changing our beliefs we can change ourselves.

Do not be afraid

REMEMBER

- You absolutely must clearly define your goals, otherwise, you will expend a lot of energy achieving nothing
- All successful people share one thing in common they defined and set themselves goals
- Without a goal, what are you going to aim for?

CHAPTER 3

ACTION

When you think back to your school days, how much do you remember? I am sure there are certain incidents, people and teachers who stand out, but I wonder how much of what you were taught has stuck and stayed with you to this day. I had a keen interest in science though I do not truthfully remember a great deal of what I learned. However, I do remember Newton's Third Law which famously states, 'for every action there is an equal and opposite reaction'. That means energy never disappears, it just changes its form. I have found this is true in life. When you take action there is always a subsequent reaction.

When you observe people you know who do not appear to be making progress in their lives – who are stuck in the same rut, repeating the same habits – and examine what is going wrong, you will very likely reach two conclusions. Either they are taking no action at all, or they are misdirecting their energy into the wrong actions. To succeed we need to be moving in the direction of our goals. This is done through the completion of the smaller goals, which you will have carefully defined and planned to complete within a specific timeframe. As a result of your planning you will have identified the actions you need to carry out and you can gauge their effectiveness as you move towards your major goals.

Many people have dreams and goals, and that is as far as it goes. They have the enthusiasm of the convert. Zealous in their determination to succeed they write a plan. Then nothing happens, because they simply do not take any action. They are like the person who, having bought the book on health care and dieting, reads it and continues eating the wrong things. Your plan is only as effective as the action you take.

When all is said and done, there is too much said and not enough done.

Anon

Our actions breathe life into our plans, yet so many people do not take action. Why not? Are the majority of people simply lazy? Do they believe that their dreams will never be realised and therefore their actions will be a waste of time?

I believe that the majority of people do not take action either because they lack the knowledge they require, or because they have too much knowledge, which ironically makes the task ahead more daunting as your understanding of what might go wrong increases and attention becomes focused on failure.

Knowledge is not power – applied knowledge is power

No matter how thoroughly we plan and prepare for what lies ahead of us, until we act nothing will happen. And when we do? How often are the initial actions, the first steps we take wholly inadequate, how often have you failed in your first attempt and immediately given up believing it is your destiny or that no matter what you do you will never succeed? When I talk to people who have given up on a goal or not taken any action at all, there is never a shortage of excuses. Some are good and most are valid, but they all seem to have missed the lesson. Having taken action that did not work, they have concluded failure to be inevitable or, with their self-confidence undermined, decided to give up rather than risk failing again. What they don't do is seek to learn the lesson from the failure.

WHY DO PEOPLE FAIL TO ACT?

The most common reason that people fail to act is they think they have got all the time in the world. It is one of the great self-administered conspiracies. We actually fool ourselves into believing that we can do it tomorrow – or next week or next month. When we tell ourselves we can do it next week, we really mean it, but when next week comes we postpone it again. Procrastination is such an invidious force. It lulls us into a false sense of security. It allows us to believe that we have not given up, we are simply 'postponing'. The actions we should be taking are *here* and *now*, not tomorrow – because as is so often the case tomorrow never comes. This is especially true when applied to changing job, or starting a health regime. Few people say, 'I'll start tomorrow', and then proceed immediately to write a plan. What they do is select a vague unconnected landmark event; at the beginning of next month, once they have moved house, or settled in to a new position at work.

Action seems to follow feeling, but really action and feeling go together; and by regulating the action, which is under the more direct control of the will, we can indirectly regulate the feeling, which is not.

William James, American philosopher and psychologist
(1842–1910)

The most common time selected is New Year. As we have all at sometime made a New Year's resolution, we will be familiar with this scenario. We decide to get fit after the season of excess. We will wait until we are back in the work routine. Then we wait until payday to join the gym. Then one day we become aware that we are getting breathless going up a flight of stairs, New Year is coming round again, and all we are is older and even less fit than before.

Postponing and procrastinating becomes a habit and is something you will not even be aware you are doing. People are trapped in patterns of behaviour that block their growth. If that sounds like you, then I have this advice for you: stop stalling, and determine to take action.

The second reason people do not take action is fear of failure. This fear is something we have learned – which means it can be unlearned. Consider how successful we were as young children: we learnt the most complex skills by a process of trial and error, with the encouragement to try again and again. Our failures were learning opportunities, and so we tried again without fear.

I have always thought the actions of men the best interpreters of their thoughts.

John Locke, English philosopher (1632–1704)

The third reason for inaction is that people have limiting beliefs that paralyse them. Deep down in their subconscious minds they believe there are things that they just cannot do, no matter how hard they try. You won't see it in children, but later in life, if we fail or are misunderstood we can convince ourselves that the task is beyond us. Instead of trying again, we simply say, 'I can't'.

I know people who tell me that they cannot cook or learn a foreign language. They have said it so often that it has become their belief. A small voice keeps reminding them, 'you can't', so they do not bother to try. The thinking that got them to this situation is dominating their expectation.

Until you break this cycle you are going to keep repeating the past. If you continue to procrastinate and stall from taking action, then you cannot progress.

The majority of people fundamentally do not believe they can change (there is that old word 'belief' again). Deep down inside they hold to a vision of the person they believe themselves to be, and live their life in a comfort zone of safe familiarity. It gives them a security blanket to wrap themselves up in. They can console themselves that they are no worse than other people and their life is not going backwards. It is not going forward either.

The fourth reason for inaction is a dominant memory of past failure. A past failure has been so painful that people now associate taking action with the pain of failure. To protect themselves from that pain the mind tells them that if they do not take action they cannot fail.

These four factors can be overcome. Those who continually put off action, focus on the difficulties, ruminate on the past and – most importantly – don't believe that they can succeed, will find that although they may have defined the goals, and they wish sincerely to achieve those goals, deep down inside, their lack of self-belief traps them in their comfort zone.

THE COMFORT ZONE

Staying in the comfort zone of life is painless, like sleep. It requires no effort, we can continue to do what we have always done; time passes, no risk of failure, no challenge of belief and no lessons to learn. When we see others passing us by, we can assume that they just got a lucky break.

Nothing happens until you take action

Without faith in ourselves our dreams become nothing more than forlorn wishes that late in life will come to haunt us, as unrealised goals, things we could have done, should have done, if only we'd taken action.

Do you know anyone who has talked for years and years about doing something or going somewhere – to fly an open cockpit plane, to run with the bulls in Spain, to climb a mountain, to sail an ocean, or have a family – goals achieved by many but things they never did? Instead they spent a life of wishing, talking and waiting for it to happen.

Earlier, I identified two types of people: those who talk and those who do. Those who talk have wishes and nothing to show. The people who do have something to show are the ones who take action. Every action creates an outcome; you are closer to your goal, or you are further away from it. If the action brings you towards your goal repeat it. If your action moves you away from your goal, learn why it did not work, and try something else.

History is full of people who have followed a vision, a goal. They did everything possible, they worked as hard as possible, 18-hour days, seven days a week, year in year out, and they finally made it. Often people hearing of the achievements of others will assume it was easy for them because they had a unique talent or opportunity. Make no mistake: they had a burning desire as well. But above all, they took action and did it – every step of the way.

Don't be too timid and squeamish about your actions. All life is an experiment. The more experiments you make the better.

Ralph Waldo Emerson (1803–1882)

When we see others who have succeeded, we rarely see their journey. Every journey, no matter how long or short requires that we take steps, continual steps. Think of each step as a contribution to your future success.

Often the mistake made is thinking of action as being something big and dramatic. We talk about real action people, we describe films as being action-packed, and we associate action with dramatic changes – not so. Reaching the South Pole or climbing Everest is a series of very small determined actions that grow in stature over time. Step after step.

You have to know what you want out of life. I have worked with clients over the years who have expressed their ambitions, and some-times they have expected I would provide some powerful wisdom that would motivate them into action. I didn't give them a magical sound bite of profound wisdom. What I did do was help them define their goal, to break it into smaller steps and make them commit to take action. Each time they completed one of their steps, I reminded them to reward themselves, to feel good about themselves, and in so doing change their self-image and face the next step with increased confidence.

I am often struck by how those who break their goals down into a series of planned steps, who stick to the plan and focus on the immediate actions, accelerate their progress towards their goal at such a rate it has even taken me by surprise. I know people who have achieved their six-month goal within three weeks. What had happened in each case was a personal transformation. Their self-image changed dramatically and they saw themselves as achievers, as opposed to non-achievers. Small successes had given them confidence.

We may take the same journey but our experience of it will always be different. With each step forward, with each small goal achieved, our confidence grows, our self-image becomes more positive, and we feel better about ourselves

Sometimes when we take a determined action we can create outrageous results. I remember many years ago I was playing golf with my father. I had never managed to beat him and we were playing the last hole. The match was all-square, but he had taken two shots and was still short of the green, and I was on the green in two shots. I was going to win. He used a pitching wedge to play his third shot in the rough some 50 yards from the pin. The ball landed on the green, ran up, hit the flag and dropped into the hole. I thought it was outrageous, I could not believe it. My first ever victory over my father cruelly denied by a ten thousand to one shot. I remember saying to him, 'You are so lucky, I can't believe you did that'.

He looked at me with a big smile and said, 'Robin, what do you think I was trying to do?'

Naturally enough he was trying to hole the shot. It was a ten thousand to one shot, but it was what he was trying to do, and by going for it, against all the odds he got it.

I once walked seventy-two miles across Scotland in under two days to raise money for an orphanage I supported. After eighteen hours on the go, I reached a particular landmark and sat down exhausted. I had covered about forty-four miles and had twenty-eight left to go. The problem was badly blistered feet and complete exhaustion. I looked in the direction of the next section and all I could see was a huge mountain ahead of me. It seemed just too much for me, given I had been on the go for eighteen hours. Then I saw a large boulder 200 yards away, so I determined to make reaching that boulder my goal, and off I went. When I reached it, I picked another spot 200 yards ahead and set off towards that. I continued to do so for the rest of the day to my finishing point twenty-eight miles away – 200 yards at a time.

Few people set goals, fewer write and create plans to realise their goals, and fewer still take action.

Men acquire a particular quality by constantly acting a particular way . . . you become just by performing just actions, temperate by performing temperate actions, brave by performing brave actions.

Aristotle (384–322 BC)

Some years ago it was estimated that the average adult watched three and a half hours of television per evening. When you watch television your brain pattern is very similar to when you sleep, which means you are not really thinking. Nothing much is going on, but you are relaxing: it is a very comfortable state to be in. I have done it myself and I am not standing in judgement of anybody, but think what this really means. Three hours a day, for just five of the seven days of the week, equals fifteen hours a week, 60 hours a month, 700 hours a year. What could you achieve in 700 hours if you took action? It would take you seventeen, 40-hour weeks to work 700 hours. Imagine you applied that time to taking positive action towards your goals in life. How much could you improve your ability to become a DIY expert, or to learn a language, or to become superbly fit and run a marathon? How many hours training do you think it takes to get yourself in great physical shape? Time is a precious commodity, and we waste it because we believe we have so much left, when in truth we do not. Take time to read books and to learn and apply the knowledge. It is good to socialise, to see your friends and pass time, but I think your life should be made up of more than passing time.

> You get out of life exactly what you put in. Put nothing in, you will get nothing out

A guitar teacher once told me that a very well-known soccer player came to see him, to learn how to play the guitar. The teacher gave a virtuoso demonstration of what can be done. The footballer, a world-class player for one of the top teams in Europe, was overwhelmed. He exclaimed, 'Will I ever be able to play like that?'

The teacher replied, 'Are you good at football?'

'Yes, I am very good.' was the indignant reply.

'Were you born a good footballer?'

'No, I worked my socks off, as a boy I practised as much as I could, I put everything into it.'

'To be great at the guitar is no different,' explained the teacher.

You cannot have a proud and chivalrous spirit if your conduct is mean and paltry; for whatever a man's actions are, such must be his spirit.

Demosthenes (384–322 BC)

But so many people are too impatient, they want it now. We live in a culture of instant gratification; whatever we want, we want it now. 'I do not want to do the exercise, I want to get one of those electronic muscle stimulators. I don't want to lose weight the hard way, I want to take magic pills that I saw advertised on that late-night programme.' There are no short cuts. What you put in is what you get out. I am talking about effort, energy and action. Make it happen, do not wait for it to happen. Be proactive, not reactive.

> Taking action does not guarantee success, but not taking action is a certain guarantee that nothing will happen

Think of it in terms of being in a car. There are two positions in that car, you can be a passenger or you can be the driver. If you are a passenger you will go where the driver takes you. If you are the driver, you determine where you are going. If we have no willpower, we will react to how we feel, let our instincts drive us and our minds wander. Our instinct takes us to our safe comfort zone. But if your conscious thought is the driver, you can determine where you are going and the speed of progress.

You really can change your life and make things happen, but it is your responsibility to take positive action and make it happen.

REMEMBER

- Nothing changes until you take action
- Always take positive steps towards your goal and the change will begin to happen
- If you fail, then learn from the experience don't identify with it

CHAPTER 4

ATTITUDE

Our attitudes are mainly acquired through life experience, the influence of other people and our own expectations. If our expectations for life are pessimistic – that bad things are likely to happen and that success will elude us it is more than likely a consequence of having developed a negative attitude. If our expectation is that good things will come our way and that we will succeed in life, then this optimistic view will be the consequence of having developed a positive attitude.

Research has indicated that people with a positive attitude tend to consider themselves to enjoy good luck, while those with negative attitudes believe themselves unlucky. This becomes their expectation. If you expect something good to happen, your interpretation of events will align with your attitude.

The greatest discovery of my generation, is that a human being can alter his life by altering his attitude of mind.

William James, American philosopher and psychologist
(1842–1910)

The majority of the skills required for success in life are attitude-based. Here is an exercise to put that to the test. Spend some time with friends, or colleagues discussing the qualities you believe you need to be successful in life or business. The list might contain skills such as communication, determination, focus, motivation, knowledge, application of knowledge, learning, empathy, compassion. Now split the list into two categories. The first category is of technical skills – that is, those that you can only acquire through conscious learning or practice, such as technical knowledge and practical skills that you have to acquire externally. The second category is larger skills which are in fact attitudes. Generally we find that about the 80% of the skills required for success will be identified as attitude-based and only 20% as technical skills. Attitude has more impact on outcome than technical skill. Technical knowledge and skills are essential, but on their own will never be enough.

A Matter Of Choice

You were not born with your attitudes formed, you acquired them from the world around you, from your parents and carers. If your mother or father had particular attitudes and expectations it is likely that your beliefs will reflect those influences.

> Your attitudes are a reflection of your beliefs

Have you ever been checking on to a flight when the customer at the counter next to you starts getting involved in a very long discussion about seats, upgrades or excess baggage? They're being stubborn and are not listening to reason. It is a situation over which you have absolutely no control. The check-in assistant is doing her best to handle it by remaining calm and not getting upset. The customer is getting more and more frustrated, continuing with their unrealistic demands. Meanwhile the queues on either side are moving at a steady pace. Let's imagine the passenger next to you is a classic negative attitude personality. They complain to you about how ridiculous the situation is. And then start getting angry. They just gave control of their response over to their emotions, thereby losing control.

> Destiny is no matter of chance. It's a matter of choice. It is not a thing to be waited for, it is a thing to be achieved.

William Jennings Bryan (1860–1925)

The negative expectation is, 'I always get in the wrong queue; this always happens to me, it's not fair'. If the passenger has a positive personality type, they too will feel equally frustrated, but will recognise that there is nothing they can do about the delay. They will either stay calm and strike a relaxed conversation with someone in line or they will choose to move to another queue. They will take control of the situation. The person who has got angry may think they have taken control but in reality the situation has taken control of them.

> The strongest principle of growth lies in human choice.

George Eliot, English novelist (1819–1880)

In life we will suffer numerous setbacks. At these moments attitude can be our greatest friend or our greatest foe. If we have positive attitude and suffer a setback, we put it into perspective, we say to ourselves, 'That wasn't what I expected, but I'll not quit.' We are able go forward again with an expectation and intention of being successful. With a negative attitude, when things go wrong the response is, 'I knew this would happen'.

I am always amazed how people give up when a project starts to experience unforeseen difficulty. Once it fails they will say, 'Well, I never really thought it would happen, I didn't believe it was a good idea. I hoped it would work out, but, I never thought it would.' The positive person by contrast is surprised when a project fails and will want to know why it failed.

BE AWARE OF YOUR ATTITUDE

Are you aware of your attitude? If you recognise that yours is negative the good news is you can change it. You can change your attitude in a heartbeat by developing a positive expectation, using positive language and become a positive person. You were not put on this earth to be miserable. You were not put on this earth to walk around gloomily expecting the worst. You have choice and in changing your life, it is a prerequisite that you change your negative attitudes to positive ones.

> Your attitudes are a product of the way you think. You create your attitudes, and apply them to your goals and expectations in life. Be under no illusion: though you may not be aware of it, you choose your own attitudes – and you can change them

In a moment of calm reflection look at yourself and your life and ask yourself this question, do I expect the best or do I expect the worst? And if you can answer those questions honestly, you have your answer. Expecting the worst equals a negative attitude, and expecting the best equals a positive one.

Is that too simple? All you need to do is to look around at your friends, the people you know and consider successful. Remember, success is having what you want in life, not simply acquiring wealth. Look at the successful people you know; those who are happy, who are fun to be around, are content, and have fulfilment. Are their attitudes positive or negative?

You Can Be In Control

Your attitudes are totally under your control. The majority of people do not seem to realise that fact. They come up with the old excuses, 'I can't help it, that's the way I am'. It is a great mystery to me why people choose to get angry as often as they do. Most people would say they do not choose to be angry, something happens that makes them so. 'I am not responsible. Blame the idiot at the front of the queue, it's not my fault I'm angry. It's their fault'. Reflect on this. Who made that person angry? They did it themselves – but they do not know it. It's their instinctive response when they do not get what they want, but it does not have to be that way.

> You can't have a positive attitude and be miserable the two states are incompatible, if you are miserable, or negative check your attitude

So let's go through what happens in a logical sequence.

Stage one: something happens.
Stage two: you interpret the event.

Stage three: the situation is analysed and filtered through your beliefs and attitudes.

Stage four: you have an emotional response.

Stage five: more likely than not, you express it in a physical reaction, you get upset and angry.

That sequence of one to five takes place in milliseconds. It happens so quickly you do not realise it is going through a process of stages. It happens so fast that you do not understand that your attitude has hijacked the situation and influenced your response. It's the same reason that when somebody does something that makes you angry, you say 'they made me angry'. But they did not, you have interpreted the information and applied your negative thinking which is 'it always goes wrong for me', 'I'm not lucky', 'it's not fair' – all aspects of a negative attitude. To convert this you need to actively re-include your attitude into your thought process. You must actively engage your attitude so that when something bad happens, you remind yourself that you are a positive person, that what is happening may not be under your control, but that your thoughts feelings and attitudes are. You make a conscious decision and tell yourself, 'I'm not going to let this upset me and I'm certainly not going to let this make me angry'.

So let us try and be clear. Your attitude is something you have; it is either positive (good), or negative (bad). If it is negative, make a conscious effort to change it. If it is already good and positive – excellent, keep it that way.

Human beings, by changing the inner attitudes of their minds, can change the outer aspects of their lives.

William James (1842–1910)

Your life will change much more quickly when you apply the outlook of a positive attitude. For once you so choose it becomes natural to take the actions that will make yourself and other people feel positive.

THE EMOTIONAL RESPONSE

Your given emotional response to any situation is a product of your beliefs. I have spoken to people who tell me stories of disillusionment and disappointment; 'My life is hard.' 'I had bad teachers, they didn't encourage or support me.' 'I went to college and my tutor didn't listen to me.' 'I went to work and I found my boss to be difficult.' 'I worked for a rubbish company, then I moved to another business and they turned out to be not much better'. They protest over the whole injustice of it all – that life is not fair, and that they were unlucky. They are wrong on all counts. Life didn't just happen to them. By not acting positively they interpreted their situation to fit in with their beliefs and attitudes. Accept that what happens in the future is the outcome of what we create here and now.

> Control your attitude and you control how you think and feel

Athletes who have been successful have an expectation of succeeding. They visualise winning, they have a positive attitude towards themselves, their abilities and the future outcomes of races they will be competing in. Successful people have a positive attitude and their beliefs and attitudes determine their expectations. And there is an inevitable ripple effect. If your expectation is success and you believe you are moving towards it, then in the present moment you will be positive, proactive, engaged and you will engage others.

> If your attitude is negative or you believe you are a failure, you will interpret everything that happens to you as a validation of your attitude and your belief

A young man plucks up the courage to ask a girl out, but he does not believe she will say yes. He takes a deep breath, expects the worst, walks up to her and he says, 'Hi, I wonder if you'd like to go out sometime soon'. 'No' she replies, 'I'm sort of seeing someone at the moment'. The man, somewhat embarrassed and tongue-tied, takes the longest walk in the world – the walk of rejection. The conclusion he draws is of great importance to his confidence and future expectation. Likewise the conclusions you draw from your experiences are central to the way you see yourself, and that is why being positive helps maintain a healthy self-image and being negative has the opposite effect.

THE DOMINANT ATTITUDE RULES

You will believe what your dominant self-image holds to be true, so if the young man believes he is unattractive he will use the rejection to strengthen that belief. If he had a positive attitude, he would still have keenly felt a sense of rejection, but would have accepted the refusal and not thought any less of himself.

Challenge what your expectations are and the assumptions you make in life. If someone says no to a proposition they are saying no to the proposition. It is not a personal rejection. If you have given someone good reason not to like you, resolve it, make it right. If they do not like you for reasons beyond your control, get on with your life and do not worry about it.

My life is an indivisible whole, and all my attitudes run into one another; and they all have their rise in my insatiable love for mankind.

Mahatma Gandhi (1869–1948)

Be in control of your attitude. Understand that attitude accounts for 80% of accomplishments in performance. It is infectious; it influences other people. When your attitude is strong, confident and positive, you will influence other people without even realising that you are doing so. The research into luck says there is no such thing as luck but only random events that occur in our lives. How you interpret these events is up to you.

Your attitude is more important than your intelligence. Positive people look for solutions and negative people look for more problems. Even when they get the right solution, they think they were lucky. You create your own good fortune in life. The key to your ability to change your life lies in your ability to master your attitudes. Choose positive attitudes, and your journey through life will be full of more happiness, laughter and hope.

Our attitude towards life is reflected in the way that life treats us

REMEMBER

- You are in 100 per cent control of your attitude
- 80 per cent of the skills you require to be successful in life are attitude-based skills
- Just always have a positive attitude – it is that simple

Chapter 5

Persistence

There is an old Chinese proverb, 'Fall over seven times, and get up eight times'. The core message of the proverb is, persist. The number one reason that businesses fail is that they do not keep up with their customers. As another old adage states, 'If you don't keep up with your customers, somebody else will'.

> People fail quite simply because they give up and stop trying – mostly just after their first setback

The average child falls over 240 times whilst learning to walk, and every time it falls over it will get back on its feet until it can walk. The child gets encouragement from the parents and from the small progress made at each attempt. You never hear a child say, 'I can't'. Children may often not want to do something but when they put their mind to achieving a goal, they will continue with persistence until they succeed.

> Failure is our teacher on the road to success

Too often in our lives we experience failure and we see that failure as absolute proof that success was never meant to happen, that we ourselves are not capable of succeeding, and that therefore it's OK to give up.

We give up on our goals because somewhere along the way we stopped believing in ourselves, or we stopped believing we were capable of achieving. It is easy to give up when you believe you cannot succeed.

I meet people from different walks of life, rich and poor, accomplished and unaccomplished. I have met people from different ethnic and religious backgrounds, all with different life experiences. I conclude that the ability to be happy, successful and fulfilled in life is not dependent upon the environment in which you grow up. Of course environment has an influence especially in the formative years, but the successes of people I have met demonstrate that as an adult you can set your own goals and by persistence achieve almost anything you put your mind to.

SUCCESS LIBERATES

Personal success is not easy but once realised it is immensely liberating, fulfilling, and joyful. To achieve we must persist through the failures, the challenges of life and the setbacks we encounter along the way. It is not enough for us to wish, to want or to desire. The world is full of people who wish, want and desire things. Until they take action nothing can happen. Some actions will lead to failure. Your desire to succeed must be driven by an unquenchable passion for the goal you have set yourself.

They who lack talent expect things to happen without effort. They ascribe failure to a lack of inspiration or ability, or to misfortune, rather than to insufficient application. At the core of every true talent there is an awareness of the difficulties inherent in any achievement, and the confidence that by persistence and patience something worthwhile will be realised.

Eric Hoffers, American social philosopher (1902–1983)

It is important to set a worthy goal for yourself, something which inspires you, which fulfils your sense of well-being, a goal which makes you feel good about yourself and will benefit your life and those of people around you. When you have such a goal, you will naturally have the commitment necessary to persist against adversity, to get up every time you fall down.

Success will follow failure. I do not know a single successful person who did not experience failure. Failure is not your enemy; it is a good acquaintance to know. Along our life journey we meet many people who are neither friends nor enemies; they are simply acquaintances who act as guides, who give us information, encouragement, or point us in the right direction at a critical junction, when we are uncertain of what to do. Failure should be seen in the same light. There is always a lesson to be learned from it. If we learn the lesson and continue on our journey, that shows a spirit of persistence.

Persistence demands that we break the negative habits of a lifetime: habits we have held on to and that have made us who we are. If you suffer the frustrations of a life you neither hoped for nor actively chose, it is essential to break those habits

If success is the goal; if fulfilment, joy and happiness are qualities in life we wish to have then why exactly do we give up on our dreams, our hopes and aspirations? It is because quitting is probably the easiest thing we can do. Quitting is effortless; it takes us straight back to the comfort zone where we feel safe, secure, with all the familiar emotional connections. After only a short time, we are ashamed that we quit. Our shame we have learnt to live with.

We sabotage ourselves, usually unconsciously. Halfway through a get-fit campaign we go away for a week. We eat, drink and forget the exercise routine. When we return we think, 'Well, what's the point, I was never going to succeed anyway'. Success is not guaranteed, but failure is. Persistence will eventually overcome failure.

People of mediocre ability sometimes achieve outstanding success because they don't know when to quit. Most men succeed because they are determined to.

George Herbert Allen, American football coach and
executive (1922–1990)

When you are on that break with friends, and you are trying to get fit and stay in good shape, think before you drink the extra beer or have the cheeseburger and french fries, 'Will this action take me closer to fitness or further away from it?' Your ability to persist in staying the course will make all the difference.

> When our belief in failure is greater than our belief in success we quit

For most people giving up is too easy – they are comfortable with the feeling. They have done it many times before and the world didn't come to an end and this time will be no different. And the comfort is reinforced by postponing the effort and convincing themselves that 'I can do this again later on'.

True, you can always start again, but if you have a habit of giving up it is most likely that the next time you begin, you will repeat the pattern of behaviour that got you to give up in the first place – and you'll give up again. We become masters of deceit in our own lives. We justify our inaction or readiness to stop trying, and we come up with excuses as creative and magical as any ever written and the only person we are damaging and letting down is ourselves.

> Happiness and success are not accidents of birth nor are they just lucky occurrences. They are the results of committing to and following through on the things you need to do

STICKING TO IT

Successful people have this in common quality, they never give up. They never accept defeat; they believe, no matter what, that there is a way, and that if they try for long enough they will find it. There are photographs taken of mountains many years ago that were classified as impossible to climb. Yet people found a way to climb them. They found routes up the most difficult mountains in the world; they found a way. There is always a way, but it comes from staying the course and persisting. The Wright brothers, the first men to fly, were bicycle engineers. They had a fascination for the concept of a flying machine heavier than air. They wanted to soar like a bird through the sky. With the passionate belief that it could be done, they set about creating the first aircraft. They didn't limit their dream by simply accepting that they were only humble bicycle mechanics, rather than qualified aeronautical experts. The accounts of the hurdles they faced is quite staggering. More often by trial and error they overcame the barriers and failures. Aeronautical science can now explain what they did. But no science can explain persistence

Fight one more round. When your feet are so tired that you have to shuffle back to the center of the ring, fight one more round. When your arms are so tired that you can hardly lift your hands to come on guard, fight one more round. When your nose is bleeding and your eyes are black and you are so tired that you wish your opponent would crack you on the jaw and put you to sleep, fight one more round –

remembering that the man who always fights one more round is never whipped.

James J. Corbett, American boxing champion (1866–1933)

Winston Churchill knew what persistence was about. He led Britain through some of the darkest moments and he is remembered for many wonderful speeches. I think it is was in his last public speech that his wisest words were uttered, when speaking to the pupils of his old school. After a long and slow walk to the dais, he looked sincerely at the boys and said, 'Never give in, never, never, never give in'.

> The lesson in adversity has been to persist. Defeat is never final until you accept it. Do the thing you love and persistence will be as natural to you as breathing. You will persist without realising it, for love is never a chore

Look back over your own life for examples of your ability to persist. No matter what your situation, I guarantee you will find moments when you did something against the odds because you stuck to it, you persisted: you overcame a challenge or an obstacle. Remember those moments. Your ability to persist needs to be intelligent because while we learn many lessons in life from our failures, we can also learn much from our successes.

Look at a stone cutter hammering away at his rock, perhaps a hundred times without as much as a crack showing in it. Yet at the hundred and first blow it will split in two, and I know it was not the last blow that did it, but all that had gone before.

Jacob A. Riis, photographer and writer (1849-1914)

BELIEVE THERE IS ALWAYS A WAY

Believing there is always a way is important in life. We should be inspired in life by our heroes. Read the life stories of those who have found success and achieved great things. If you get a chance, write them a letter and ask them how they did it. You will find time and time again it comes back to desire, because when you have the desire, you will have the determination to commit and persist.

> You only fail in life when you quit, and only you choose the moment at which you quit

You will discover that the people who achieve great things are no more special than you, no more talented. They are no more unique than you. They have their own qualities, as you do also. We are limited by our physical abilities, and for that reason we cannot all be world champions in golf, athletics or formula one racing. But what we can do is become the best that we can be. That should be our aspiration, to be greater than we are and to reach the heights of our own abilities. We will never do that if we do not challenge our abilities with persistence.

If you wish success in life, make perseverance your bosom friend, experience your wise counsellor, caution your elder brother, and hope your guardian.

Joseph Addison, English essayist and politician (1672–1719)

REMEMBER

- Never give up, just persist, and learn from your mistakes
- People don't fail because they are unlucky they fail because they quit
- Defeat is never final, until you accept it

CHAPTER 6

FEAR

Fear is powerful emotion. It can paralyse us; make us stop in our tracks. Fear of failure and fear of rejection are the two most undermining emotions in life, though these fears are often irrational and without grounds. They focus on an outcome that has not happened and may never happen, yet it exists firmly in the mind.

Fear kept early man alive – it is a useful emotion. It heightened his senses when competing for food and shelter. It is quite natural to be afraid of falling, afraid of death, serious injury, disease or hunger; of things that threaten our lives. But the emotions and responses we associate with fear have now found their way into other areas of our life that do not endanger our survival, but do threaten our sense of security. We are afraid of rejection and of failure. Rejection and failure are not life-threatening. Yet approval and acceptance have become so important to our lives they have become our dominant motivation.

Fear is a negative attitude. People who are worriers and pessimistic about life in general tend to be of a negative disposition. People with a positive attitude are less fear orientated. They look for the outcomes. They focus on their goals. People who are fearful focus on seeking approval and avoiding risks.

A life lived in fear is a life half lived.

Anon

Entrepreneurs are people who take risks. They have a goal, a vision of an outcome they wish to achieve. It becomes their focus. Taking risks is not about being reckless. It is a considered choice. It is trusting in one's own self-worth and ability. It is taking action knowing that a goal will be achieved, or that greater understanding will be obtained through setbacks on the way.

OVERCOMING YOUR FEARS

Most of the things we fear are never going to happen

To overcome our fears we need to deconstruct them. There are two categories of fear we have in life. Those that are rational – fear of death, fear of serious injury, serious illness, fear of poverty; and those that are irrational ones – fear of failure and fear of rejection. The rational fears help us survive. The irrational fears we have learnt and absorbed into our thinking. We were born virtually fearless. Scientists believe that even the only two fears in newborn infants – of loud noises and of falling, are learnt in the womb and in the very first days of life.

As children we get ourselves into all kinds of risky positions. We climb ladders without a safety harness; we eat food from the floor or the dog's bowl – without asking the dog's permission first. Much of what we do is based on ignorance. We have no reason to think there is something wrong. We learn fear from others; we acquire them mainly from our parents. 'Monkey see – monkey do.' If our parents express a fear, even if it is slightly irrational, we learn that fear, we put it into our memory and it becomes part of our beliefs and attitudes.

Fear is the enemy, it robs you of confidence, desire, commitment and hope. Beat it down and break through its illusion.

The fears that people have, they learn. If they dwell on them they magnify them by their imagination until they become phobias or superstitions. I have heard that many student doctors and nurses start believing that aches, pains and freckles they have not noticed before are in fact skin cancer or some obscure deadly ailment when studying major illnesses and infectious diseases. Many of these students go through a stage of hypochondria because fear of death and serious illness is very powerful and by focusing their attention on their fear they convince themselves that they are about to die.

CHALLENGE YOUR FEARS

When we experience fear, our irrational beliefs so dominate our thought process that we focus on the outcome we dread. In the case of our fear of failure, our rational thought process is so undermined that the fear is used to justify the belief and attitude, and we say 'I can't'. We are paralysed by our own beliefs, attitudes and intellect conspiring against our desires.

Do not fear life, as you do not fear the stars or the evening breeze. We are all here for a purpose and everything happens for a reason.

Unknown

Of course, while too much fear can be debilitating, not enough fear can be equally dangerous because when you are completely fearless you become reckless. Not only do you endanger your own life but also the lives of others. I do not want a reckless pilot or taxi driver who knows no fear, one who believes they are immortal, or believes in some misplaced sense of destiny that all will be okay. Fear serves a purpose when it is rational.

> Challenge your fears, and see if they are real or illusory. Does what you're frightened of exist in reality or only in your mind?

The way to overcome your irrational fears is to challenge them, deconstruct them and then replace them with choice. You need to focus on the outcomes you want. When you catch yourself responding automatically to a situation with 'I can't', or 'It's impossible', visualise the desired outcome, the fearless outcome. Now engage your intellect, before your beliefs and attitudes kick in, in visualising the next step towards your goal.

You can change your life when you change the way you think; this is the recurring message throughout this book. As long as you believe you cannot change the way you think, you will not. But I promise you, you can, it is a choice you make.

Habits are formed through repetition, which is why you have to visit the goals and the positive outcomes you seek every day, even every hour if need be, to visualise clearly what you are aiming for, to see yourself successful. Visualise yourself as having achieved your goals, see yourself in a situation you have previously found fearful and now see yourself succeeding and not being afraid. As Winston Churchill said most of the things we worry about never come to pass. Most of your fears are irrational and unlikely ever to happen. Fears tend to be about future events, not the present moment. You need to experience the present, be aware of the here and now, and then you can take positive action.

Fear is the number one obstacle to success. Fear is the reason people do not take action. The unconscious belief is: as long as you do not act you cannot fail. Your fears can remain ignored, subtly controlling your thinking, or you can control them through thought. As the American President Franklin Roosevelt said, 'We have nothing to fear, but fear itself'.

> The opposite of fear is not courage. The opposite of fear is confidence

Fear will make you stop. Confidence enables you to move forward; to have a go, to do your best; to test your ability. Confidence is about having faith. When you have confidence in others, it is because you trust them and believe that they will act in your best interest.

No passion so effectually robs the mind of all its powers of acting and reasoning as fear.

Edmund Burke, British politician and writer (1729–1797)

MEET YOUR IMAGINED FEARS HEAD ON

One of my fears has been the idea of free fall parachuting, yet at the same time I am fascinated by the thrill of the activity, and the thought of flying. From childhood it had been an ambition of mine, but equally it had been a lifelong fear. The idea of jumping from a plane and the parachute not opening was the most awful thing I could imagine. Now proportionate fear of having an accident is rational enough, but an overwhelming sense of parachuting being something that I could never ever do is not. Though no one can guarantee that the parachute will open perfectly every time the statistics tell us that it is a safe sport, with many safety features built into the equipment and rigorous training drills. So learning to skydive was top of my 100 things to do in the next ten years. I just found 101 other things to do first instead.

Three years ago, whilst travelling across Montana, I discovered there was a skydive school located 40 miles from where I was staying. So I bit the bullet, confronted my irrational fear and I called them up. I signed up for a four-day course. On the day I was due to start, I went to the airfield early and sat in the car waiting for the airfield to come to life. Then the worries started. 'What if the parachute doesn't open?' 'What if it was badly packed?' 'What if the plane crashes?' 'What if my instructor blacks out in mid air?' 'What if I'm overcome by fear and freeze?' 'What if I die?' Slowly but surely my confidence – what little I had – drained away.

Fear had come home to roost. I started the engine and drove off, telling myself that I would do it another time, another place. So I did what so many of us do: I had a little conspiracy with myself that I was not really quitting, I was not really being afraid, I was being sensible, I was resetting my time frame. Deep down inside, I knew that fear had overcome me. I had walked away from one life challenge that I had desperately wanted to meet.

A few hours later, I was still telling myself I had made the right choice, but I decided it would be discourteous of me not to phone the skydive academy and apologise. No sooner had I got on the phone than the instructor said.

'Robin we were so looking forward to seeing you, you were one of our few customers today.'

I was so embarrassed. I said I was sorry but something had come up that made it impossible to get there. I did not add that it had been my breakfast. The lie sounded anything but convincing.

'Well, Robin, come tomorrow. We won't have time to teach you to do the full skydive course in three days, but I can do a tandem jump with you. I'll strap you to my chest and we will jump 13,500 feet. You will love it.'

The next morning, after a sleepless night, I arrived at the airfield. I was so nervous that I could feel myself physically shaking. The instructor smiled. I cannot remember if we exchanged words. I signed the various forms disclaimers, next of kin – then the fee plus an additional $50 so the whole event could be recorded on video.

After twenty minutes of ground instruction, we walked towards the aircraft. As we were about to board the instructor said, 'Remember, Robin when we climb out on the wing at 13,500 feet, with our feet on the wheel plate and holding the wing strut, I want you to do two things. First, I want you to look at the cameraman and smile, and, second, I want you to enjoy yourself'.

We flew to 13,500 feet. Then we moved out onto the strut, into the position before we let go. I remembered to look at the camera and attempt a smile – which start to finish I think lasted less than one fifth of a second. And then, we launched ourselves into space. We were in freefall for about 30 seconds before the instructor deployed the parachute. The cameraman was waiting for us as he had landed before us. He ran up and said, 'Robin, that was a great skydive, how did you enjoy it?'

I had no opportunity to view the video until I returned home, and as the format was American I had to wait a few more weeks before I managed to get the tape converted to the UK video format. So weeks later when I finally saw the video. I was amazed by my reply to the cameraman. I said, 'Boy, when I left the aircraft, I wasn't afraid. I could have stayed there all day. I thought I was flying'.

Once I left the aircraft I left my lifelong fear behind me, jumping wasn't dying – it was flying.

Most of the things we fear in life are illusions that exist only in our imaginations, and the more we think about them the bigger they get

A year after that skydive in Montana, I had still not fulfilled my ambition of doing it myself. I still had a fear. So I set about deconstructing my fear. I read up as much as I could about skydiving and talked with people who jumped every weekend.

The knowledge gained helped me to deconstruct my fear. Parachutes fail, of course they do, they are mechanical, but it is extremely rare, and in any case you have a reserve. With this fear in perspective I then started to visualise my skydive. Knowing the procedures I would undertake, I visualised every part of the process. I signed up to do a course. I spent a day training. The weather at the end of the day made it impossible to make that first jump. I wasn't too unhappy – I had been nervous throughout the day. They told me to come back another time to make my first descent. Weeks passed, in which I again put it off several times.

Do the thing you fear and the death of fear is certain.

Ralph Waldo Emerson (1803–1882)

At last one Saturday evening, knowing the weather would be perfect the next day, I determined I would make my jump. The next morning I woke at 5.30 and drove to the airfield. I signed up for a jump. I had to take a few tests. I got kitted up, put my parachute on and waited to board the aircraft. I had gone over this so many hundreds of times in my mind I knew exactly what was happening. A very strange thing happened. I found a sense of calm came over me. I was not afraid. I was, however, very aware of what I would be doing and what I would have to do. We climbed to the height, to 13,500 feet. The instructor turned to me and asked, 'Are you ready to skydive?' I'd been told during the training that this question is asked to every first-time student and was the last opportunity for the student to back out if they do not feel ready. He told me it is quite naturally a very nervy time, and apparently most students barely manage to squeak a 'yes', on account of the nerves making their mouths so dry. My instructor told me he was always keen to hear something a little more original, which had been occupying my thoughts on the ascent.

So when we got to 13,500 feet and the instructor tapped me on the arm and said 'Are you ready to skydive?' I shouted over the engine noise, 'Born ready, what are we waiting for?' We went to the door and as taught I went through an exit count and we left the aircraft. I made my first free fall parachute jump, pulling my own rip cord. I had overcome a lifelong fear by visualising the goal and the experience, deconstructing the fear, and living a dream.

> We can live our dreams if we can identify our fears, deconstruct them, and replace them with positive thoughts of success and feelings of happiness

We often mistake our irrational fears for rational fears, and our first response to fear is to run – to give up. At the end of our lives we will not regret the things at which we failed. We will regret the things we wanted to do but were afraid to do. The reality is, where challenges were not life threatening, that we chose to be afraid.

> When you overcome your fears you will open up a world of possibilities that you never imagined could be yours

Most of the fears we have in life are of things that have not happened and probably never will. So focus on the things in your life that you want to happen, and not on the things you fear. They are only in your imagination. Put something else there, something else positive, and remember that the thing you think about is the one you move towards.

REMEMBER

- 99 per cent of the things you fear, are never going to happen
- Recognise that most fears that hold you back are imagined, and exist only in your imagination
- To overcome your fears does not require courage, it requires personal confidence

CHAPTER 7

FAILURE

We seek to avoid failure at all costs. Yet in doing so we miss out on valuable life lessons.

We are exposed to approval and failure early in life. We seek our parents' approval, then as we go through life it seems as though most scenarios we encounter have a pass or fail outcome. We go to school and take tests which we pass or fail; we apply to college and must pass at a certain grade or fail to be admitted. Whatever the test – be it for a driving licence, a job interview, or meeting our girlfriend's or boyfriend's parents for the first time – we want to pass, just as we want approval. The alternative – failure – is painful, and a rejection. In fact as people go through life, they define everything by these outcomes. Their world is made up of winners and losers, with failure being the enemy. They need to lighten up. And of course not assume that if they fail then it automatically follows that they are failures. The truth is only that they have had an experience in which they met with failure.

> It is the very experience of failure that enables us to move in the direction of our success

It is natural for us to want to avoid failure, because it may make us feel down, or we worry that our self-esteem will suffer a blow, or we believe that others will judge us as less capable than we would wish them to think we are.

> Many of life's failures are people who did not realise how close they were to success when they gave up.
>
> *Thomas Edison* (1847–1931)

A LESSON FROM SCHOOL

Think of people with dyslexia, who frequently experience difficulty in reading because of their word blindness. However intelligent they are, if their condition goes unrecognised by the education system, they can seem to be poor students who fail to keep up with the rest of the class. They can easily fail formal examinations, given their reading difficulties. Yet it is obvious that they are not in themselves failures, which suggests that we need another perspective on what constitutes failure: not a formal exam that you flunk but a life unfulfilled.

I was interested to learn that people with dyslexia are four times more likely to become self-made millionaires than those without. So the school measure of their ability to succeed in examinations was no indicator to their ability to succeed in life. In fact, because the formal written route was not easy for them, they learned how to express themselves orally. They learnt how to create inspiring images in the minds of the people to whom they were speaking, and to overcome challenges as they met them.

When you fail it is critically important that you recognise you are not a failure

FAILURE IS NOT PERMANENT

If we choose to see ourselves as failures, our self-esteem suffers accordingly, and the outcome of our endeavours will align with that belief. History records that many successful discoveries were the result of countless previous failures by inventors or scientists who did not give up. When an experiment did not work out as planned, they looked for the reason why; then they applied what they'd learned to the next experiment, and tried again, with no certainty of success, only the belief that they were moving in the right direction. They did not give up. Our lives are works in progress towards our life goals, and will in the course of our learning about ourselves be full of trial and error. While learning to walk we had to fall over. While learning to speak we had to be misunderstood. While learning to dance we had to step on toes. With the confidence of youth, we did not identify with these mistakes: we just got on with it.

Intellectual capacity is not an indicator of future life success and neither is being naturally gifted. Life success is a combination of many factors, including beliefs, vision, attitude, and commitment. However, without a strong belief in yourself, those around you will shape your sense of identity, and, experience of failure will become a dominant fear. It is vital you do not misinterpret the events around you as being indicators of who you are.

To begin to think with purpose, is to enter the ranks of those strong ones who only recognise failure as one of the pathways to attainment.

James Allen, British writer and philosopher (1864–1912)

Take victory and defeat with equal grace

Failures are inevitable in life. When you experience them, it is an experience of the moment. You need to move on – do not sit and procrastinate, or indulge in studying it too much. Learn the lesson from it, see why it happened and move on. There are many people who carry the burden of failure with them an entire lifetime, an exam failed, a relationship that did not work out. The rest of their life is spent with the words, 'if only'. They beat themselves up, day in day out.

The past has gone; it does not exist. Let it go.

SUCCESS ENCOURAGES, FAILURE TEACHES

When you have seen and enjoyed a comedian perform, it is worth remembering that you are witnessing the end result of something that started with a nervous first appearence many years before. The highs and lows of performing are so far apart that comedians use expressions like, 'I killed out there tonight' to mean they were on fire and every joke hit the mark, or 'I died' when no one laughed and nothing worked for them, a horrible experience. 'Bombing', is the ultimate failure, the audience completely silent or, worse, talking through the act or even heckling. There is a very nervy atmosphere in the comedian's room backstage. Anxieties are suppressed. Fears and worries are hidden behind false laughter. The fear of failure can be overwhelming, because when you fail as a comic there is no where to hide, you fail in full view of both your peer group, and strangers who are judging you.

Commitment and determination to succeed are what overcome fear of failure. Every comedian can talk of the 'hell gigs', the night it all went wrong. If every comic who bombed thought they were a failure and gave up after the experience, there would be no comics anywhere. But to get better and to understand their craft the comedians who bombed one night got up the next and tried again. So you too must keep trying. The fact is you are not going to win every race, every cake you bake is not going to be perfect, every golf shot you hit will not fly straight, every person you fall in love with will not love you back and every interview you go for will not result in a job.

Don't be discouraged by a failure. It can be a positive experience. Failure is, in a sense, the highway to success, inasmuch as every discovery of what is false leads us to seek ernestly after what is true, and every fresh experience points out some form of error which we shall afterwards carefully avoid.

John Keats, poet (1795–1821)

Failure is integral to our success. How can you know success without having experienced failure to compare it to? Yet for many of us it is too hard to bear. We see children inconsolable after they have lost a simple family game, losing their temper and lost in their little world, saying that it is not fair, refusing to play with another child, refusing to share their toys. Adults watching their team lose in a championship final can be in tears, distraught, though the failure is not their own. Still it's painful and devastating. Make no mistake, failure is not an old friend of mine whose company I seek to avoid as much as possible. But equally every time I have had the experience, where there was a lesson to learn, I got it, and when there was not – I moved on and got over it. Failure, like success, is an experience of the moment. Experiences do not define who we are. How we respond to them is a measure of who we are.

> Failure is only final when you accept it

We have to change our perspective on failure and see it as an opportunity, an experience from which we can learn, accepting things as they are in the moment and seeking to be more successful next time.

Success also requires you to have a positive attitude, and that you visualise your goals, which will put failure in perspective. You will see it as another event, a moment in time. When you are able to deconstruct your fear of failure, you can move on. You must always move on.

Tom Watson, one of the great golfers, was runner-up in a number of major championships. He was known as a choker: when the big moment came he would make mistakes and snatch defeat from the jaws of victory. People said he did not have what it took to be a major champion. The press were highly critical of him. But he never stopped believing in himself. He said, 'All these failures are teaching me how to win.' Eventually he learnt his lesson – he went on to win five British Open titles.

Given a choice between experiencing failure or success, make no mistake, I choose success. However, to avoiding failure at all costs deprives you of opportunities to grow as a person, to build your confidence, to test your ideas and to strengthen your abilities. I was taught to be a gracious loser. We need to keep about us a personal sense of grace, a personal sense of balance, that things in themselves are not good or bad, and victory and failure are relative. See failure as a step towards success.

> Failure is an opportunity to test your resolve, to build your determination, and develop your character

Sun-Tzu a famous Chinese General, wrote, 'Failure is the foundation of success and the means by which it is achieved'. It is important to accept failure. When you fail do not blame others as that only develops a blame culture. Do not spend your time thinking of excuses to justify failure that will reinforce failure, be gracious in your defeat, and be gracious in your failure. Learn the lesson then apply the knowledge.

> Success will follow your last failure – and that is why you must always persist

REMEMBER

- There is no failure only learning opportunities
- Failure is an experience you learn from, not a condition that afflicts you
- Better you try and fail on the road to success, than never try and regret it later

CHAPTER 8

HONESTY

Have you seen a television programme where an antiques expert examines an object and declares it to be authentic? Imitations may entertain, but it is the genuine article that holds value.

Are you the genuine article? If you're not you need to become so. To change our lives we need to be honest with ourselves – we need to be authentic. We should not be blind to aspects of ourselves that we are not comfortable with, or imagine things to be other than they truly are. In all aspects of our goals, our beliefs, our attitudes and our expectations we must be completely honest with ourselves.

No legacy is so rich as honesty.

William Shakespeare (1564–1616), *All's Well that Ends Well*, Act 3 scene v

We are not born with delusions or anxieties; we are not born greedy, vain or frightened. We acquire these traits through life experience. A parent or carer giving the message that we are good, clever, capable, brave or attractive will encourage us to use that as our template of who we are. As adults we have to examine the facts and decide for ourselves what is true. That requires personal honesty.

What you give, you get in return. If you give honesty, you will receive honesty

When people go into a court of law to give evidence they are required to swear upon a bible to tell the truth, the whole truth and nothing but the truth. The truth is everything when important life decisions are made. In our day-to-day lives we do not always tell the truth.

It is facts we must be honest with. Do not mistake opinions for facts

BEING HONEST WITH OURSELVES

Being honest with yourself is as essential to personal growth as exercise is to physical fitness

We must be honest with ourselves in the pursuit of our goals. I worked with a client over a three-month period. He told me he was doing everything he had planned, all the short-term goals had been identified, the timeframe set and the goals visualised regularly. There was no progress at all and of course I was concerned. The client decided that it was my failure – I had let him down, I had not given him sufficient instruction or the motivation to succeed. He came up with all sorts of reasons, so it was no surprise when he blamed me too. I was disappointed that he had not made progress, but intuitively I felt he had difficulty in accepting responsibility. He had been saying all the right things but doing nothing. He was also blaming his friends, his background, his luck; it was extraordinary. Then I recognised the connection between denial and responsibility. We look for reasons beyond our control, blaming teachers, colleagues, upbringing, whatever, but not at ourselves. We feel out of control. Together we were able to recognise that the client really needed to re-set his goals and start over again. He did – and at last things moved forward.

Where is there dignity unless there is honesty?

Cicero (106 –43BC)

Do you blame a diet for being too hard, or your boss for being too difficult? Do you blame the gym for being too inaccessible? Try to avoid blaming the world around you, if it is in fact your choices and mistakes that have caused the problem. Painful as it might be, understanding very accurately where you are in relation to the goals you seek to achieve is enormously important.

AVOID DENIAL

We need to open our eyes and acknowledge what is happening in our lives. We need to acknowledge what needs to be done, not to ignore things in the forlorn hope that they will just go away and be okay. If we are not making progress towards our dreams and the successes we wish for, we need to identify why not. The chances are we will discover we are not being completely honest with ourselves.

The more honest you are with yourself, the more you deal
with the facts and not what you merely imagine to be true –
the faster you will change your life

People do not wake up one day and discover they are 100lbs
overweight or that they have a drink problem. They were aware as
it gradually happened but chose to ignore it. When they drank too
much they just said it was a one-off. When they bought cigarettes
they justified it, saying this is the last packet. Being honest with
yourself requires you to take action responding to the realities of
life as it is, not as you wish it was.

All truths are easy to understand
once they are discovered; the point
is to discover them.

Galileo Galilei (1564–1642)

What happens is that most people stay in denial until there is a crisis.
Perhaps we lose our job, and suddenly realise that our attitude and
behaviour have just become so poor that people no longer want to
work with us because we are no longer contributing to the organisa-
tion. Or we get so overweight that the doctor tells us we have a
serious risk of having a heart attack. Or our smoking or drinking gets
out of hand and the damage we are doing to our bodies is suddenly
acknowledged by the way we feel, our inability to catch our breath.

When crisis occurs, people are forced to deal with reality
and take responsibility or do nothing and become a victim

I have met people who drink far too much who say, 'I don't care, I like getting drunk'. These are the expressions of addiction. Those people are in denial – ignoring the evidence – not being honest with themselves. These are the traits of addiction. This book is not about addiction, but if you recognise these traits you need to consult a doctor.

I have met people who have suffered a lifestyle-induced medical crisis. I can think of one in particular who, had serious health problems as a result of their lifestyle and who had to have major surgery. Two years later he no longer smoked or drank, had lost 40lbs in weight, and had run two marathons for charities. But why wait for a crisis? Sometimes we do not get a second chance.

Be honest with yourself and deal with facts that will enable you to make the right choices. When we lie, we delude ourselves. We hear these denials so often that we have come to accept them as reality. That is why I stress the importance of beliefs in the first chapter in Part 2. Believing what you think is true becomes reality. The more honest you can be about the facts of your life, the easier it will be to change your life.

DON'T GET CONNED

There are criminals known as 'con artists' who specialise in gaining the confidence of their victims, then separating them from their money. They present facts and figures, dates and details. They take you into their confidence with flattery and generosity. Then they tell you about an amazing opportunity to make a huge profit on some deal. It's perfectly safe: you can buy for a fraction of the value and sell on the same day for a fantastic margin. The whole elaborate premise is based upon greed and false information presented to people as paying something for nothing, or a lot of return on minimum layout. The victims do not question what is happening because they choose to believe *what they want to believe*.

When I was twenty-two I hitchhiked with a friend to India from Scotland. It was a great adventure, done on the super-cheap and by the time we got to Bombay we were exhausted and running low on funds. We were frequently approached by money changers in the street who offered a rate of exchange twice the official government bank rate. When asked how this was possible, they always had a brilliant story about avoiding unfair taxes, doing business overseas and needing foreign currency – always very plausible.

I learned many things growing up in Glasgow which have served me well in life, and a man I once worked with told me that when a deal is too good to be true – it is. So I never entertained being a part of this obvious scam. I met several young travellers who had lost all their money and were having to go home, their greed or naïveté having got the better of them. I did however with my friend decide to turn the tables on the con men.

Whenever I was approached to change money I acted very gullible. Then I told each money-changer that if he could give me the very best rate I would change $2000 – which I thought was funny as I had less than $80 to my name at the time. Having got each of them to agree to the most preposterous rate of exchange – often double what they had originally quoted – I then arranged to meet every one of them in the same hotel lobby the following day at 1pm exactly. I never found out what happened as I left early the next morning. But I would have loved to have been there, and seen them when they all saw each other.

All truth passes through three stages. First it is ridiculed. Second, it is violently opposed. Third, it is accepted as being self evident.

Arthur Schopenhauer, philosopher (1788–1860)

BE HONEST IN YOUR SELF ANALYSIS

People underestimate the downside and overestimate the up side. Doctors have told me when they ask patients how much they drink, most will estimate within recommended safe limits. Doctors recommend a limit of twenty units of alcohol per week. When the doctor asks a heavy drinker how much they drink, they will say, oh about twenty units, and yet from the result of their liver function test the doctor knows this cannot be true. Smokers, when asked how many cigarettes they smoke, say 5–10 when it is probably 10–20. The overweight when asked about exercise say they don't go to a gym but they walk a lot. They are giving the answer they think the doctor wants to hear and don't want to be scared into realising what can happen as a result of the life they are really leading.

> It is important that we extend honesty into all aspects of our life and we develop integrity. We become people who can be trusted; our word is good. When we say we will do something we do it

In the absence of honest appraisal, all we will have is assumption. How often have you assumed something incorrectly? Do you find yourself starting sentences, 'But I thought . . .'? There is an expression, 'The older I get the better I was.' I would like to change that to, 'The older I get the better I become, because I am learning all the time.'

BE CLEAR ABOUT WHERE YOU ARE

If you do not know where you are now how will you find the path to where you are going? If you are not honest with yourself, if you do not know yourself, how will you know what to do to reach your goals? When you are honest with yourself you will find out exactly where you are, and once you know where you are you will know the direction you need to go to.

> Our lives improve only when we take chances – and the first and most difficult risk we can take is to be honest with ourselves.
>
> *Walter Anderson, Artist (1905–1965)*

Today there is so much urgency in our lives: we want immediate gratification, and we want success now. But what you put in is what you get out. Too often we convince ourselves that we have the qualities and experience we need, when we haven't.

'Fake it until you make it' is a popular mantra of many personal development philosophies. This does not mean be dishonest with yourself. It means focusing on the goal you seek to achieve and acting in accordance with the belief that you are moving towards it. You are not being dishonest because you have consciously decided to change your behaviours to become the person you want to become.

You are not claiming qualities you do not have; you are trying to acquire them.

But you need to know the difference. Be honest: don't deceive yourself. Only when you know who you are and where you are can you decide what you want to be.

REMEMBER

- Honesty is the best policy
- Until you are honest with yourself then change will be impossible
- Never mistake an opinion for a fact

CHAPTER 9

LIVING IN THE PRESENT

The past is gone. Whether the past is full of trauma or happy memories it is gone, you cannot change it. The future, for all its uncertainties, does not exist. Here and now is where we are.

So many people are dissatisfied with their lives. They reminisce endlessly about how much better things were in the 'good old days'. Others set their happiness in the future, dependent on events that may never happen, or the acquisition of things they will never need.

We all do this to varying degrees. I know when I meet up with friends from my school days, we frequently reminisce about particular teachers, games, embarrassing dates, catastrophes on the clothing front, and we remember the emotions of that time. By remembering the event we recall the feelings the memory invokes.

> The present moment is where you are, and is the only time you have control over, live it well, and use it wisely

Schools and colleges have reunions, great events at which we look back and remind ourselves of our lives and the experiences we have shared with others. It's fine to live in the past for a bit, it's normal to reminisce, but it's not fine to dwell endlessly on what you no longer have.

> People who live in the past have selective memories, and fear the uncertainty of the future

When we face a challenge in life, we will go through our memory banks to see if we have any previous experience we can draw upon. The more powerful memory, the stronger the emotional connection. Unfortunately those experiences that carry a negative emotion tend to be most powerfully remembered. When we face a challenge and recall our strongest emotional memories, it is our failures we remember. That is selective memory at its most damaging.

Failure provides us with a learning opportunity. If we do not learn from failure, we are destined to recreate it time and time again. By living in the present we can focus our actions on the here and now, and in so doing learn what works and what does not. We do not have to repeat the past actions that caused us to fail.

> You can change your life – but only you can do it

Every book you read, every mentor you listen to, every course you attend will only be an enabler, not a solution in itself. Never mistake the content for the solution. You can change your life but it is important that the actions you take are rooted here and now. Do not spend time worrying about the past. Learn from your failures and move on. Do not spend time daydreaming about the future, have a plan and take action.

DROP THE USELESS HEAVY STUFF

Let us look a little deeper at why people live in the past. Why do some people spend their life bearing grudges? They hang on to anger. They hang on to a moment in their life where a great injustice was committed against them. For the rest of their life they repeat the story as they have done a hundred times before, awaiting your sympathy. They are unable to forgive, and their inability simply feeds anger. A sense of injustice can overwhelm you. You can go through life telling the world that it's not your fault you are angry. Deep down inside, it comforts you. It gives you a false sense of purpose and excuses failure.

> We can only really be alive in the present moment. It is all we have, it is where we are. The past is gone, it's a distant memory. The future doesn't exist. But it is in the present moment that we can shape our lives

Other people live in the future, eternally daydreaming. They take no action. They will tell you how if they won the lottery, they would spend the money and what they would do. I have known people who for years have told me about the business they are going to start. The reality is that taking action to start the business is anxiety provoking. So they continue to research. They go to night classes; they become authorities on their chosen dream. Tragically they cannot make that first step. The studying and all the research becomes a diversionary activity. They are having a daydream and living in the future. If they were living in the present they would see the need to take action.

This time, like all times, is a very good one, if we but know what to do with it.

Ralph Waldo Emerson, American essayist and poet
(1803–1882)

SUCCESS IS AN EXPERIENCE

Success is not the destination; it is the experience of the journey. It is the experience of the moment. Too often we make our happiness in life conditional: 'I'll be happy if I have a new car' or 'I'll be successful when I've got a management position.' In reality, your life is made up of a series of moments that blend into one continual experience – life.

> The only moment in your life you can experience is the present moment. Use it well: take the actions that move you towards your life goals

By living in the present moment you can appreciate the world around you and you can appreciate the success you have in your life. Success is a state of mind, like happiness. There are outward manifestations of success, which we are all aware of – power, cars, homes – but they do not make a successful person. Your success is found in how you feel about yourself, and how you feel about the achievements in your life no matter how grand or simple they are. When we have this appreciation of ourselves, we are fully alive. Being fully alive means appreciating the present moment.

I am always saddened by stories of those who, too late in life become aware of the wonder of life, the joy in a smile, the love of a friend, the sound of rainfall. All around us there are objects and experiences we take for granted. Have you ever stopped to wonder at how a bumblebee flies, or how a salmon finds its way back to the river of its origin? Have you ever stopped to wonder about life? I recommend you do.

> Slow down and take time to appreciate all those things you take for granted

A man became fed up with life. He was jaded. He had made money, but it brought him no happiness. He had travelled, but it brought him no joy. He had power, but he worried about his responsibilities. Deep down inside he lacked any real sense of accomplishment. He went off to see a doctor. There were no pills for his condition. The doctor told him to take a day off, go to the beach and follow the instructions in three envelopes he gave him. The next day the man went down to the beach. The first envelope had on the front the instruction 'to be opened at 9am', the second said 'Open at noon' and the third, 'Open at 3pm'.

Enthusiastically he tore open the first envelope. Full of expectation, he felt at last he was going to get some comfort, and make some sense of his life. It contained a card. There was one word written on it: 'look'. He flipped the card over looking for secret instructions or a hidden message, but it was blank; he looked around to see if anyone was watching, but there was nobody. So he looked, saw nothing, and within two minutes he had become profoundly bored. This game was no longer fun. He did not want to be on the beach because he was a busy man. But he was stubborn too and determined to stick with it. After fifteen minutes of daydreaming about work and looking out to sea he noticed the patterns that the waves had left in the sand. Shortly afterwards, he noticed a sand crab struggling up the beach. He then saw an elderly couple walk by hand in hand. Out at sea he saw a ship going somewhere. And he started to wonder about the journey the passengers were on and where they had come from. He looked down at his feet and saw the grass growing through the sand. He wondered at the fact that there was no nourishment in the sand. When he tried to pull the grass out he was amazed to discover that the roots went so deep, to get every last drop of moisture. Then he became aware of the birds flying overhead. He noticed things he had taken for granted as though he was seeing them for the first time. He looked at his watch and noticed it was almost 12 o'clock. He opened the second envelope. There was another card with the word, 'Listen'. Though he was a busy man and pretty sure he had got the point of the exercise, he decided he would do as he was told. For the last three hours he had been listening. Or at least he thought he had. Then, he heard the gulls cry as they flew out to sea, he caught snippets of conversations as people walked by, and he heard the sound of the wind blowing through the grass. He realised that if he could get close enough he would probably hear the noise the sand crab made as it burrowed into the sand. And then he heard, for the first time in his life, the silence. That moment between any noise. He had been aware of silence, but he had never heard it before, in that space between sounds when the mind is free of thought. It was the most beautiful sound he had ever heard. He realised that he had stopped thinking and just sat in silence looking and listening. He found the third envelope. He could not imagine what could be written in this third envelope so he started to think about it. What would this last word be? Would it be 'walk, talk, think'? He couldn't imagine. Now relaxed, he opened the final envelope and there was written, 'Enjoy'.

Life is divided into three terms – that which was, which is and which will be. Let us learn from the past to profit by the present, and from the present to live better in the future.

Anon

We look to the past and remember the good old days, but were they really the good old days or are we just remembering through rose-tinted glasses? The big mistake we make is that we tend to selectively remember the good bits. We end up thinking the best days of our lives are behind us.

Remember, 'today' will be one of the good old days we will recall in years to come. Success is a here and now experience. It should not be conditional on a future event or compared to our past, because this blinds us to the opportunities of the present. Take time to experience life all around you and be conscious that the decisions you make will influence the outcomes you experience.

> Life is to be enjoyed, yet we spend so much of it running busily around, paying no attention to the most important time in our lives: now

Most people like familiarity, they like routine in their life, it gives them a sense of security and well-being. When we are consciously in the present moment we may become aware that past behaviours are inappropriate. To change from previous behaviours that have become habits can make us uncomfortable. When change comes along in our lives and we have no control over it, it makes us anxious or insecure and we respond by resisting. At work have you heard somebody say, 'Why do we have to do it this way, I liked the old way?' Better or worse, who knows – it is just another way of doing things.

Success and personal development require you to visualise what you want and believe it will come to be. This is not suggesting that you just think it and it will magically appear. Rather, by being consciously aware of the present moment and creating a sub-conscious image of a future event, your subconscious mind will look for the opportunities that will help you enable the process to happen in the here and now.

You must live in the present, launch yourself on every wave, find your eternity in each moment. Fools stand on their island opportunities and look toward another land. There is no other land, this is no other life but this.

Henry David Thoreau (1817-1862)

> When you are with someone, be with them fully. Don't look over their shoulder at whoever else you could be talking to, or speak only with the hope of gaining some benefit from them. Give them your full attention; make eye contact; smile. Make them feel good about having met you. Make that moment in their life a good moment

As you go through life you have a choice, to look for the positive or look for the negative. Make an effort to make people smile. When I have a short encounter with the check-in attendant at the airport, with my dentist or my godson Charlie, with people I meet throughout the day, I make a point of smiling positively. If that sounds a little deliberate, try it, and then let me know what you think. I have come to realise that the present moment is the only thing we have. I may never see any of these people again. Some I am sure I will never see again. So I want to treat every moment with someone as though it were the last time I will ever see them. I want that moment to be as good as it can be.

Life is made up of moments. It is not made up of things

Often we think that if we possess things we will have joy. The truth is that our lives are a collection of moments that will be what we remember at the end of our lives. A moment can be a smile, a pat on the back or a quietly spoken 'well done'. It can be a sunset admired or flower in full bloom seen as though for the first time. It can be a perfect silence. The more moments you can create in your life, the greater your life experience will be. To appreciate the moments live in the present. Do not carry unnecessary emotional baggage from your past. Do not spend your life daydreaming about a future that you are not taking action to create. Do not make your happiness conditional on future circumstance. Be aware of the here and now. Your actions in the present moment affect the future. You will find that good cause will create good effect.

My favourite moments are ones of uncontrollable, joyful laughter. I cannot plan them, I cannot get in my diary and say that next Wednesday at six o'clock I will have a moment of uncontrollable laughter, but when it happens I become fully aware of that moment and I savour it.

We don't receive wisdom; we must discover it for ourselves after a journey that no one can take for us.

Marcel Proust, French novelist (1871–1922)

Participate in the good. Observe and experience the bad and learn from it. We need to have a child-like quality to be aware of the present. When children are playing they are completely absorbed in what they are doing; a piece of string and a piece of paper can become two marvellous toys in their hands. They are totally engrossed in the present moment. They are not watching clocks or remembering the past. They can have a little fight over something, but five minutes later it is forgotten. They are like the wolf in Part I: who if you asked it the time, would say 'It is now'.

It is quite natural to remember past failures and to revisit memories of happiness. When we are in the present moment and experience it to its full, then we will understand the past as a series of moments that led to the here and now. We learn its lessons and move on encouraged by our memories of joy.

Sometimes living in the present can sound a little bit impractical. People will tell me that they do not have the time to meditate, to visualise. But time passes, and the only time that we really have in our life that we have any control of is here and now. So do not waste it.

REMEMBER

- The present moment is where we create the future
- Don't live in the past, or worry endlessly about the future
- Make the most of here and now, and in so doing you will be open to opportunities and experiences

CHAPTER 10

PATIENCE

I was watching a comedy show on television in which a group of protesters were carrying banners and marching outside a gate. The leader of the protest had a megaphone and he was chanting into it, 'What do we want?' The group chanted back, 'Don't know!' He continued, 'When do we want it?' and they all shouted, 'Now.'

Many of us do not truly know what we want and yet have a strong feeling of dissatisfaction. We feel life can be a lot better – and indeed it can. It is paradoxical that so many people want happiness now, yet so few can define what that happiness actually is. Yet until we know what it is, it will remain impossible to realise.

Life has speeded up: we live in a consumer culture where we no longer wish to be kept waiting. The emphasis is on things becoming faster and more immediately available to us when and where we want them. That is fine within the commercial arena. But as individuals we need to learn consciously to slow down, we need to manage our time, we need to create calm in our lives and stay connected to it throughout the day.

> Never lose your patience when events beyond your control slow down your progress. Stay calm, use the time to think about other things you want to do in life. You will discover time moves more quickly when you are patient

Imagine you are in the queue at a supermarket checkout, and the person in front of you does not have sufficient funds to pay. The manager is called and a discussion ensues. When this happens how do you feel? Do you think to yourself 'Why does this always happen to me?' Do you feel victimised?

At such moments we lose control of our emotional response to the situation, and our feelings go through frustration to anger. We get angry, particularly with the person who is slowing us up, and start complaining to the other people in the queue. We allow the situation to take control of us and dominate our emotional response. And yet, we can control how we react to the situation by the simple application of patience.

PATIENCE IS A VIRTUE

Patience means to endure. Endurance can imply either hardship, or something supremely noble. Patience allows us to be calm in a moment, by making a conscious choice to be relaxed and not let the situation dominate how we feel. Patience is an attitude, one we can acquire. We can choose to be a patient person. It takes practice. It is a habit, which you can form. Amongst its many benefits, it allows us to stay in control – and keeps our stress levels down.

Without patience it becomes easier to give up when we encounter situations that are beyond our control, that frustrate us. Sometimes we need to let events unfold and respond to what happens. It is of no use to work ourselves into a state of anger, frustration or rage because we cannot control a situation. It is best to be relaxed and to be calm.

Consider the hourglass; there is nothing to be accomplished by rattling or shaking; you have to wait patiently until the sand, grain by grain, has run from one funnel into the other.

John Christian Morgenstern, poet (1871–1914)

How often in our lives have our emotions got the better of us? Failure comes along and we get frustrated by our lack of success at even the smallest things. Rather than being calm and taking stock of the situation, our emotions take over when really we need to be aware. I am sure we have all had this experience at some time.

> In the face of repeated rejection, our ability to remain calm and unperturbed, to demonstrate patience and take action will give us the strength to go on

I think that, because we live in an 'instant' society we have lost the ability to be patient when things don't go as we expected, and as a result we simply get stressed. We believe life is not giving us what we are entitled to.

> Patience is not something you are born with; it is a habit you develop

By learning to be patient, we can avoid those feelings of anger and stress that accompany the experience of not being in control or being a victim of a situation. The reason many of us feel impatient can be traced to early childhood. Then we got more or less instant gratification: when we cried, we were fed; when we hurt ourselves, we were picked up and comforted. Our needs were met at once. For many of us that expectation never goes away.

If I have ever made any valuable discoveries, it has been owing more to patient attention, than to any other talent.

Isaac Newton (1642–1727)

Nelson Mandela spent over 10,000 days in jail, much of it in solitary confinement. When he came out of jail in 1990, he did not have hatred in his heart. He had not spent all the time in jail being angry, frustrated and bitter. I have no doubt there was sadness at being apart from his people and unable to serve them, but he said, 'man's goodness is a flame that can be hidden but never extinguished, and I believe in all of us, there is hope. For many of us it has been reduced to such a small light we have lost touch with it, but when we can apply patience to the belief in our ability to succeed with hope in our hearts, we can continue'.

We all encounter situations, people and events for which we have little tolerance. When this happens we respond emotionally with fear, jealousy or anger. By stepping back from these emotions and understanding that our beliefs and attitudes influence our emotions we will allow ourselves the opportunities to be in control.

We have no problem showing patience to those we love. With an elderly parent walking slowly down the road, or a child trying to read, it is no effort to be calm and quietly encouraging. And yet so few people can be truly patient with themselves. Is it that we do not love ourselves or do we not believe we deserve the affection for ourselves that we show to others?

The most important relationship you will ever have in your life is with yourself. You must learn to like and love yourself, and respect yourself. You must be good to yourself, look after your body. You must spend time getting to know yourself. This might mean taking walks in the morning by yourself, spending quiet time in the here and now. It means being totally relaxed and being comfortable with who you are. And when a stressful situation arrives, you can coach yourself into being patient and let the moment pass.

Patience serves as a protection against wrongs. So you must grow in patience when you meet with great wrongs, they will then be powerless to vex your mind.

Leonardo da Vinci, engineer and artist (1452–1519)

PATIENCE IS A CHOICE

There is order in the universe; there are natural laws, which dictate how the universe operates. We are part of the universe and are affected by those laws. If we take action, we create an effect, though the time it takes for the effect to be felt is not always known to us. If we sit in silent frustration because things are not happening fast enough, we will only cause ourselves unnecessary stress. We do not know how long things will take to manifest themselves in our lives and that is why a calm sense and a personal endurance will enable us to avoid irrational knee-jerk reactions.

Many wrong choices, even though they feel right at the time, can be made in an impulsive moment. Patience is a choice, an attitude. We are capable of changing our life when we change our beliefs and our attitudes. We can choose patience, and in the process avoid the damaging effects caused by being in a stressful state and at the mercy of negative feelings.

> When I was diagnosed with cancer, I had to go in to the hospital for a series of tests so that they could determine how advanced the cancer was. I had to undergo a procedure called a lymphangiogram. A lymphangiogram is when they make small incisions on the tops of both feet and a very fine needle is placed into the lymphatic system, through which dye is sent. The dye goes into your lymphatic system and an x-ray is taken, which will show up if there are tumours. It is a very exact procedure because the lymph vessels are so small and fragile they break very easily. Inserting the needle is a tricky process. The nurse came into the room and prepared me for the procedure. I remember lying there nervously, I did not know what the results were going to be. The nurse had made incisions in both feet. She struggled to get the needles in position, and after half an hour had passed, I was very concerned. I desperately wanted the needles in place so we could find out exactly how far the cancer had spread. And then a profound sense of calm came over me. I told myself not to worry: 'This will pass and it will be fine. If it doesn't work, I'm sure they'll think of something else.'
>
> At that moment a young doctor came in and asked the nurse how she was getting on. The nurse told her it was tricky. The doctor offered to try, leant across and put the needle straight in. Even she was surprised with the ease with which she did it.

I learned many things while I was being treated for cancer. It is very natural to worry when you think you may be dying. I'm not suggesting for a second that my just being patient and calm suddenly made everything OK. What I did find was that I could stay more relaxed. I could listen more attentively and respond more effectively. By being patient I did not get frustrated with the treatment, I did not get angry with the experience. I was able to be more participative in my treatment. I was not a victim with no control.

Patience is not about abandoning ourselves to the twists and turns of an uncertain future, rather it is about hope because in the absence of evidence, hope is all we have. We need to have a patience that allows us to keep hope alive in our heart

Adopt the pace of nature: her secret is patience.

Ralph Waldo Emerson (1803–1882)

If we can practise patience, we will discover that other qualities in our life improve. It has been my experience that patience and humility go hand in hand: practise one and you develop the other. Research has indicated that children who can delay their pleasure and demonstrate patience have less trouble with stress in later life. As children we find it very hard to sit still – I am sure you remember somebody saying to you, 'Stop fidgeting'. Yet as adults we find it very hard to do nothing, unless we are in a waiting room or a dentist chair.

Try this exercise: sit in a chair and do nothing. No book, no television, no music, just silence, just sit in silence. You may find yourself getting frustrated, you may feel you are wasting time, that you could be doing something much better. I want you to sit there. I want you to sit there and do nothing. Do not try to meditate, do not close your eyes, do not try to relax, just do nothing and be comfortable with doing nothing. Become aware that if you choose to, you can be relaxed doing nothing. Sit in your chair, do nothing and be comfortable with that moment of inactivity. Recognise that you can choose to be frustrated by the experience, or be calm.

The great faiths understand the power of patience. In Buddhism, patience is one of the ways to enlightenment. In the Koran, it is identified as one of the 99 divine attributes of the almighty; and in the Bible, the story of Job recommends an enduring patience and devotion to God in the face of trials beyond human comprehension

You need to practise patience. It is not about giving in, or opting out, or losing. It is about choosing to wait in a state of calm, about allowing yourself to understand that any emotional response that is not constructive is not worth making. It is a time to reflect and to live in the moment, ready to act when you choose.

I do not think patience comes to us naturally. It is a habit, which can be acquired. I marvel at cultures which seem to have the habit built in. At a railway station in India I once asked somebody when the train would be coming. They looked, smiled and said, 'Soon.' People were sitting around cooking meals, relaxing, having a siesta. No one was marching up and down, banging on the window of the ticket office. No one was complaining to the driver when the train finally arrived, or when it made an unscheduled stop for ten minutes so people could get out and pray. In this culture patience is a way of life. Make no mistake, behind the calm and the patience there is determination and commitment. It is just they do not allow themselves to get frustrated at things over which they have no control.

There are many things that will happen to you today over which you have no control. When stressful situations occur, practise patience. There will be times in your life when you are awaiting a vital decision or news. When your nerves are taut, feelings are running high and butterflies are flying formation patterns around your stomach, getting stressed is not good for you and won't affect the outcome. Your ability to be patient will not affect the outcome either, but it will allow you to remain calm and relaxed and more able to cope with life.

REMEMBER

- Patience is an attitude and a habit that you can acquire
- Stay calm as much as you can, otherwise your emotions will end up controlling you
- In times of hardship and disappointment your patience will enable you to put it into perspective, and remain in control

CHAPTER 11

HUMILITY

Humility is a virtue. It is the opposite of arrogance. It is the absence of a need to be self-important. Humility allows us to go through life without needing to see ourselves as better than others. Humility is accepting, it is quiet and it is calm. Humility is a confident respect for others and for oneself.

Arrogance is the assumption that we are better than others. It is an unfounded belief that we possess qualities we do not have, thus giving us a false sense of confidence or superiority. When people become self-centered they become unattractive.

Almost every religion preaches the notion of non-attachment: not to be attached to things, to objects, to other people, and ultimately to ourselves, or life itself. We need to be free of illusions about ourselves and the world: humility can help us.

Humility does not mean thinking less of yourself than of other people, nor does it mean having opinion of your own gifts. It means freedom from thinking about yourself at all.

William Temple, English statesman and author (1628–1699)

Over the years I have tried to identify the qualities that enable us to be our best self. I have tried to understand the age-old question of why some people go through life with a cheerful and joyful disposition, while for others every day is a struggle for happiness, self-acceptance and feelings of personal worth. Many successful people are described as having larger-than-life personalities, many celebrities are better known for their need for attention and their demands than for their professional skills. If there is no correlation between who we imagine ourselves to be and how we are seen, we become crippled by the need to be someone we cannot be. We stop being honest with ourselves, and our sense of self-worth becomes dependent on others and on material things. To avoid this we need to overcome unfounded self-importance, we need humility in our lives. It may appear as a quality reserved for saints, mystics and history's heroes, but it is not – it is a quality that will help us grow.

> You may seek fame or power, but they will not change who you are; they do not give you anything substantial. For ultimately the key to happiness is found only in who you become, and not in what you have

Being driven by status and power can turn normal people into unattractive, vain, demanding and tempestuous people whose company we avoid. These people feel the need to be recognised, the need to be important. They see themselves as better than others. By thinking you are better than another person, or that your position is more important, you give yourself a false sense of who you are.

Humility is the foundation of all other virtues.

Saint Augustine (354–430AD)

Humility allows us to appreciate life. It allows us to celebrate life, because we no longer need to judge other people, or compare ourselves to them. When comparing ourselves to others it is possible that we make a value judgement, and as a result feel superior or inferior to them. Naturally I hope that you feel equal to them no matter who they are, but people often judge themselves against others' wealth, status, beauty or whatever else they use by way of comparison. When we feel superior it creates isolation, false emotions and assumptions. When we feel inferior, it creates confusion, disillusionment and depressive emotions. Either way neither of these are good states to be in.

> Humility has no need to impress

Humility enables us to be fully open to others, to really listen to them, to give them all of our attention, because we no longer worry about what they may be thinking about us, nor are we judging them.

Humility is not about putting yourself down, or seeing yourself as less capable than other people. Humility frees us from the desire to be important. Have you ever met somebody who had a very high opinion of themselves, was arrogant, vain and conceited? Did you warm to them; did you want to become their friend? Did they make you feel good? When you spoke to them did they give you 100% of attention?

I believe that humility gives us a sense of peace and calm that enables us to be open to the experiences of life, to meet people as they are. And it may also go a long way to explaining a person's success.

> People will forget what you say, but they will never forget how you made them feel

BE RESPONSIBLE FOR YOUR ACTIONS

So many of the messages we get today suggest that it is a cruel, dog-eat-dog world and that you should look out only for yourself. This belief breeds egotistical, selfish, self-centred behaviour. I do not believe the pursuit of success demands that we have those qualities. I do not believe that we succeed at the expense of our humanity or that we should go through life hurting others emotionally and making them feel less able, simply because they are competitors.

> In peace there's nothing so becomes a man as modest stillness and humility.
>
> *William Shakespeare* (1564–1616)

Everything you say and everything you do has the power to make another person feel good or bad about themselves. It is your choice. When you have an ego that is demanding or in pain, if you are insecure or feel bad about yourself or just plain grumpy, you will pull others down to your level of discomfort and suffering. If you are secure, at ease with yourself and have no sense of self-importance it is likely that you will lift them up. We all have a sense of self-worth but being important is not our goal. Being happy and successful is. People who pursue power and wealth, because of the status it gives, may find recognition. The most important recognition you deserve is your own. Recognise your uniqueness, your qualities, your talents and your skills. Demonstrate them through action and deed and not through posturing and position.

To be successful you do not need to demonstrate humility – the person who is egotistical and the person who is humble both have equal chance to achieve success. But there is a difference. I think the egotistical person will have a completely different perception and experience from the person who is humble.

As we go through this journey in life we should try to do so with humility, seeking not to be the centre of the universe, just a part of it

REMEMBER

- Be yourself, the only person you need to impress is yourself
- Our lives are not measured by what we make, rather by what we become
- Humility is not a weakness, on the contrary it is a strength

CHAPTER 12

LOVE

There are many definitions of love. For some it is a matter of the heart that relates to human relationships and manifests itself in romantic attachments. For others it can be seen in affection or desire. And yet many people spend their lives trying to find real love. Love does not deconstruct into component parts, it is either present or it is not present.

When talking about the importance of life and living it as richly and fully as possible, I can only share my experiences. I do not want to be dogmatic or prescriptive. I do however want to share my understanding of the aspects of life that are part of the richness and fulfilment that we seek.

UNCONDITIONAL LOVE

I believe that the purpose of life is the pursuit of unconditional love, that when we discover it, we discover our oneness with the world, and with each other. The most important relationship that we ever have in our lives is the relationship we have with ourselves. Not that we should love ourselves based upon some narcissistic ideal or that we should simply think we are wonderful. It is a case of accepting ourselves as we are, and loving that person. Until we are able to accept ourselves, and to love ourselves, it is difficult for other people to accept or love us.

Life without love is like a tree without blossoms or fruit.

Kahlil Gibran, poet and philosopher (1883–1931)

Without love, life can be a lonely, desolate place and we cannot grow to the person we wish to be. The traumatic effect on children who have been brought up in isolation in orphanages is well documented. I cannot imagine anyone who was not moved by the horrendous scenes of emotional deprivation and hunger that greeted the Western press when they were taken to orphanages after the fall of the Ceaucescu government in Romania in 1989. We need to experience, share and have love in our lives.

Likewise, when we set goals, it is infinitely easier to endure the challenges and hardships they pose if we are doing something which we truly love, because we know we are moving on to a future that engages us both emotionally and spiritually.

To love someone deeply gives you strength, being loved by someone deeply gives you courage.

Lao-Tzu (570–490BC)

I am not suggesting that you shave your head and become a mystic on a mountain top, nor that you become a hopeless romantic viewing the world through rose-tinted glasses, blind to reality. Rather I would suggest that you have a passion for your life, the people you meet, the experiences you have – and feel that they are interconnected. To be fully alive in the moment you must feel connected to the world and for that reason it is very important that the goals you set yourselves and the actions you take are for love and that you love to do them.

Life is a challenge – Meet it!
Life is a song – Sing it!
Life is a dream – Realise it!
Life is a game – Play it!
Life is love – Enjoy it!

Unknown

I read an account of a supermarket in America that hired a young man with Down's Syndrome. His job was to pack bags at the checkout. Everyday he turned up on time, and was as helpful as he could be. At first many of the customers avoided his queue because they were uncomfortable. The young man made a point of putting a little inspirational quotation into each bag, as a thought for the day. The manager noticed that people would go out of their way to stand in the line where he was bag-packing, even though other lines were shorter. Why was this? That young man's love for his job, enthusiasm, the smiles he gave the customers, his cheery hellos and the little thoughtful notes he put in their bags were appreciated. He loved what he did, and that love became manifest in his work. His obvious love for what he was doing made people feel good, and was fed back to him in their appreciation.

Religious writers and mystics often come to the conclusion after many years of thought, meditation and study that God is love. Some people might be uncomfortable with that idea. Some associate love with relationships and emotional stress. For many people belief in a God is something they are not comfortable with or they simply do not accept. I am not interested in convincing people of what I believe. I do wish to share what I understand to be true.

WHAT YOU GIVE YOU GET

There is a natural law of reciprocity; what you give in life you get back. If you give out kindness you will over your lifetime receive that kindness back, often in ways of which you may not be fully aware. The same is true of love. When you give love unconditionally, then love will come back to you in many simple forms.

> Love is a canvas furnished by nature and embroidered by imagination.
>
> *François-Marie Voltaire, writer* (1694–1778)

Have you ever helped a stranger, someone who needed help? A car has broken down, a person has too much baggage to carry, or somebody is struggling with a problem, and you acted simply to help or encourage them? Why did you do it? What were you feeling when you did it? What benefit were you trying to give? Did you think any of these things when you went, intuitively, instinctively to their assistance? I doubt that you made any conscious calculation. I believe at the root of such actions is just love.

Love heals

BE YOURSELF

You may not have turned out the way your parents expected and your lifestyle may not fit into that of the world around you, but that does not make you a less worthy person, less able, or less deserving of your own love and the love of those around you.

Loving yourself and accepting yourself does not happen immediately. You need to make a conscious decision to change. This means you need to start believing you are good, that you are worthy, that you are capable of loving and being loved. Do not base your self-image on false information. Look in your life for reasons, acts of kindness and generosity. If you look you will find much evidence that you have shown kindness and love towards others.

Love is not simply the declaration of a feeling or intention. We cannot walk around all day with flowers in our hair, singing songs and showing the world that we are a loving person by our attitude or dress; it has to be demonstrated by our actions. When you have true feelings of love in your heart, then your behaviour and your actions will reflect them.

> Life's greatest happiness is to be convinced we are loved.

> *Victor Hugo* (1802–1885)

You live in the real world; you know that no matter how hard you work, and how kind you are to others, there are people to whom it will not make a jot of difference. There are people who will show no gratitude, never say please or thank you, never acknowledge a kindness or a helping hand, who feel that it is their right. Even so, when you give love there is always a reaction, though you may not see it at once.

The first girl I truly loved in my life dumped me. She told me that I could not afford to give her the life she wanted, the life her mother had enjoyed, and she left me. The comedy circuit for me was not too lucrative. I was heartbroken, did not eat, and lost weight, just like the best drama characters do. The lesson I learned much later is that love is unconditional. You cannot put a condition on it. In life we all deserve to be loved unconditionally and true love is unconditional, irrespective of somebody's size, shape, age, weight, ethnic background, prospects, potential, or the car they drive.

> Love is only worthwhile when it is unconditional. It is not measured by what we get out of it, or put into it. It is liberating when it is freely given and freely received

When we act from love we give freely of ourselves. From love, comes kindness, compassion, generosity, understanding, passion, romance, forgiveness, patience, acceptance and many wonderful qualities.

LOVE IS OFTEN HIDDEN FROM VIEW

Every adversity has a benefit in our lives. Often at the time it is impossible to comprehend the lesson. I can think of no greater adversity than the loss of a loved one, the death of someone close to us.

The death of my father was the first time I experienced such a loss; I was distraught. He was my friend, a good man. From his death I learned a powerful lesson, that every relationship we have is important, that time is precious. It may seem obvious – but it is amazing how many obvious things we can be blind to.

When I was diagnosed with cancer, I was in the Royal Marsden Hospital awaiting the results of many tests and under-going treatment. There I learnt how much I was loved by my family and my friends. I also truly understood how much I loved them.

Following the death of my father, I went into a slump. It was a painful and confused time for me. I failed my exams in my second year and left university. The experience made me examine my life and ask the question, 'What do I really want to do?' Rather than choose a career defined by academic ability, I knew deep in my heart that what I really wanted was to be a comedy writer. My greatest pleasure had been in writing and performing university shows. I chose to pursue that career with success until the diag-nosis of cancer, when life once again forced me to re-assess.

> Do the thing you love and persistence will be as natural to you as breathing. You will persist without realising it. Love is never a chore

A farmer in Scotland lived in a house about 300 yards away from the main road, down a dirt track. Following illness, his wife had been confined permanently to a wheelchair and the vehicle required that would allow her to travel in her wheelchair would not fit down the path. The farmer applied to the local council for grants to put a proper roadway into the existing pathway and was told it was not possible, it would cost too much. It was suggested they sell the farm and move closer to the town where the services they require would be more accessible. They had lived there all their lives and the farmer decided he would build the road himself. Every morning he got up an hour and a half earlier than normal to dig and lay this road, and when he came back from the fields in the evening, he would once again go out and work long into the darkness. It took him well over a year, but he built a perfect road, by hand. He dug it out, he widened it, he shored it up, he levelled it, he rolled it, and the vehicle to take his wife to and from the hospital could now be bought for them to travel in. It was an act of persistence inspired by love and devotion.

SIMPLE ACTS OF LOVE AND COMPASSION

A former soldier I know is a very quietly spoken man who has achieved many extraordinary things in his life, though you would never know it. He never talks about himself, and is not in the least boastful. He is immensely loyal and very kind. I noticed an award from the Humane Society, on his wall one day. I asked him what it was for, and he told me that one night when he was walking home, he heard some screams and found a young man who had fallen into a river and was hanging on for dear life. My friend climbed over the bridge, scrambled down an embankment and waded out with a branch to rescue him. This, to me, was all the more remarkable because I know this fellow cannot swim, but he did not hesitate to put his life at risk to save another person.

I was once involved in organising an outdoor training event where one of the exercises involved map-reading. I arrived at the place where we were due to rendezvous half-an-hour early. The instructor I had hired was waiting for me: a very tough and scary-looking individual, but very softly spoken and friendly. While we were waiting for the exercise to begin, an elderly lady arrived in the car park to take her dog for a walk in the woods. Very casually the instructor suggested that we go for a stroll. We walked along a forest path, keeping the elderly lady and her dog in sight. Eventually, she returned to her car, put her dog in the back and drove away. As she did so he looked at me and said, 'She shouldn't be walking in the woods by herself, she could have got herself hurt. I thought it was best that we keep an eye on her.'

Both these people demonstrated simple acts of love and compassion. The motive for them did not come from a sense of reward or glory. It came from a desire to act in the best interests of another. In our own lives we can do this everyday: we can demonstrate our kindness, our compassion and our love for other people in the ordinary actions we take as well as the extra-ordinary. A smile, a good intention, a kind thought, wishing someone well and really meaning it are all simple acts of love. They are simple acts of love in action and they make a difference. We develop ourselves towards personal fulfilment when we connect with love in action.

> One word frees us of all the weight
> and pain of life. That word is love.

Sophocles, dramatist (496–406BC)

COMPASSION FOR OTHERS

Imagine you go to a party. You are mingling with a number of guests, some of whom you think look quite interesting and would like to talk to, and one or two you think you must avoid like the plague – they look like they are going to bore you to death. The host comes across to introduce you to somebody you thought would bore you to death. You have prejudged them. You do not think they can help you personally or professionally so you are not that fussed. But just before you are introduced the host takes you aside and tells you this person is terminally ill. What difference would that make to the way you spoke and how you felt about them? If they asked your help in any capacity, even if it was just to get them a drink or help them upstairs would you do it? Why would you do it?

Perhaps the feelings we experience when we are in love represent a normal state. Being in love shows a person who he should be.

Anton Chekhov, dramatist (1860–1904)

I believe you would do it, not only because it is the right thing to do, but because when the fragile nature of life becomes apparent, its true meaning also becomes clear. We realise that all we can offer another person is love, compassion and understanding.

We see the world not as it is, but as we are. We need to allow love in our life, and from love will come many meaningful behaviours and actions. Obituary columns often describe people as being good, kind, generous, philanthropic, fun, easy-going, good-natured and loving. Is there any finer legacy to leave than to be a loving person? Too often, we make our love conditional. We grew up being told that if we were good boys or good girls, then we would be rewarded. Yet parents love their children uncondi-tionally. Nevertheless some children, in seeking their parents' approval, interpret love as a conditional response to behaviour. It isn't. Love must be unconditional or it is not love.

> We must learn to be unconditional in our love, and we must look for opportunities in life to demonstrate that love in action

I believe that love should be at the heart of our actions. We should hold love in our hearts; when we help others and share what we have with them, we should do so with love. To give a homeless person some money is giving of your wealth; to spend ten minutes talking with them and finding out about them is love, caring about another person. Like the ripple of a stone upon a pond, our actions travel far beyond the point of origin, long after we are gone. The effect they have can change and influence lives in a positive way. That is why we should seek always to do the best we can and to do the right thing.

You may never see the impact your smile can have, or know the effect of your kind words to a stranger in trouble, you may never know the difference you made to a life through a chance encounter. But there will be an effect.

Clarity of mind means clarity of passion, too; this is why a great and clear mind loves ardently and sees distinctly what it loves.

Blaise Pascal, French theologian and scientist (1623–1662)

I have received letters from people who told me of things I had done for them. Things that were so insignificant to me that not only I could I not remember the occasion, I could not remember the person. When they told me of the difference I had made in their lives, I was deeply moved. One person told me that they had almost given up on life itself, and I had taken the time to write a short note encouraging them, saying I believed they could succeed. They said it was the first time in their life anyone had ever believed in them. So be careful what you say, and how you treat other people. Whatever you do and whenever you do it, do it with love.

REMEMBER

- Life is love
- What you put in to life, life gives you back with interest – when you apply love to your actions, you create meaning and value
- Don't make love conditional. True love is unconditional

CHAPTER 13

MOTIVATION

Motivation is defined as an internal state that arouses, directs and maintains behaviour. I cannot imagine that sentence throws energy through your system or makes you jump to your feet and say, 'That's exactly what I want'. However, we have to focus on motivation and see it as an internal state, a response to a situation. When people have achieved extraordinary feats of endurance, all they had to keep them going was their determination and mental state. There are stories of people who have walked thousands of miles to freedom, of people who have worked eighteen hours a day, year in, year out, to realise and achieve their goals. All they had was a belief in themselves, an attitude of success and an unshakeable conviction about their ability to succeed. It is these qualities that drive motivation.

> Desire is the key to motivation

Much research has been done into the factors which motivate individuals at work. The research always seems to end up with the same conclusion: that people are motivated to perform best when they feel appreciated and involved.

In the working environment appreciation and involvement can

be expressed in recognition from our colleagues, even by simple acts of praise. More generally we require a peer group who validate us, a collective group that we feel part of and belong to, and a shared outcome to which our contribution matters. But in the absence of a peer group we have to learn to motivate ourselves.

MOTIVATION IS DESIRE IN ACTION

I think of motivation as the force that moves us towards our goals. One famous study recognised five levels of need which motivate us. The first two were to do with basic physical survival, the instinctive motivations we all have. Breathing, eating and self-protection meet these needs.

The third was about love and belonging – being a part of a group, the giving and receiving of affection. The fourth was self-esteem – the need to feel good about ourselves and to like who we are.

The fifth and highest motivational need is called self-actualisation. In other words, even if the first four needs are in place, for people to be at peace with themselves they must be true to their own nature. I interpret that as becoming the person you were born to be – being authentic.

MOTIVATION IN WORK AND PLAY

In our work motivation comes in many forms. At an instinctive level it is fear and reward; the carrot and stick; the security of a salary and fear of unemployment. Yet the mystery of motivation is that while the studies have identified several common motivators there is no magic formula.

In the workplace appreciation and the need to feel involved are forms of collective motivation, but they rely on other people to make them work. In the absence of a support group it is possible to appreciate ourselves. I know people who say a quiet, 'Well done', to themselves when they have achieved something. When I go for a run and would rather be sitting at my desk, I will always come back and say to myself, well done, good run. I will appreciate my effort and that simple acknowledgement makes me feel good, and becomes a positive memory of the experience.

Pursue your goals with purpose and passion, and you will discover your motivation

We need motivation in our lives to keep on track towards our goals. Without self-motivation we will stay where we are, we will procrastinate and find excuses and reasons not to do things. Many people perform to the level to which they are pushed. Society or their parents push them; maybe it is their coach or a boss at work. What happens when that person is not around any longer? We must learn to push ourselves and become our own coaches, we must learn to be responsible to ourselves, and just as we will try not to let our coach or parent down, we must learn not to let ourselves down.

The peak performers in this world have all learned the art of motivating themselves. They do this by focusing on the goal, with a laser-like concentration. They keep their eye on the target, the object of desire, and do not waiver. They have their goal firmly identified in their mind and are inspired by it, it gives them purpose and meaning. They are passionate about it, and have a single-minded determination and commitment to making it happen.

We are motivated towards reward and away from punishment. So, in life, what is it that most people want? Earlier in this book I said that most people have never identified their goal. If asked, I think happiness would come near the top of any person's list. We seek happiness, we seek acceptance, we want to grow as human beings, and we want to achieve success in our life. It is so important that we define exactly what success will look like to us.

> Motivation is not about knowing; it is about doing. It is a passionate desire within you to achieve the outcome you seek

Your motivation will come from within, there is no magic pill for it. People can help you clarify your goals, identify your strategy, but they cannot give you the motivation itself. The motivation comes from your desire and that comes from within.

How often in our lives have we been forced to take action? How often have you had a deadline brought forward that you simply had to make? How often has a car broken down at a vital time and yet you managed to make other arrangements? The moment when things were not going to plan, the crisis forced you to take action.

Your motivation to do so was based on a desire to complete the task or reach your destination. Many people do not take action because no suitable crisis has occurred. They drift along in life until one day they run out of time and their dream dies.

> Show me a person with desire and I will show you a motivated person

At the end of our lives we do not regret the things at which we failed, but the things we wished for and never attempted. Yet even with an awareness of our inactivity, we still do not take action. We assume that there is enough time; we conspire with ourselves to believe it is okay and things will somehow just work out. I am sorry to tell you – they will not.

Only passions, great passions, can elevate the soul to great things.

Denis Diderot, French encyclopedist (1713–1784)

Do you remember as a child being told that you were going to visit the circus, or writing to Santa Claus a few days before Christmas, or waiting for your birthday to arrive? These were always times of great excitement. As children we could barely contain ourselves. We could not sleep the night before, we woke up early in a state of excitement, we were looking forward with anticipation to something we just knew would be wonderful and we would enjoy.

GET EXCITED

We need to get excited about our goals, to drive ourselves forward and yet be aware of the prospect of failure. We must break our goals down into small, manageable steps, and we must recognise that without the motivation we will give up. Every small goal achieved is a step that builds our confidence, builds our positive self-image, and fuels our motivation.

Self-motivation is difficult. We let ourselves down easily. We justify our inaction with a myriad of excuses. We will postpone with the notion that we can start later. We let ourselves down because that is what we have done before. Anyway you look at it, our motivation will fail because the desire behind it was not strong enough. Therefore it is important that we identify what we want. Identify the goal you seek to achieve and see it clearly in your mind, in colour, in three dimensions, smell it, touch it, see it, and when you see it you must see the benefits that surround it, you must see what achieving your goal brings you.

Until you surrender to your desire, you will not take action. Many of us have desires, vaguely identified, loosely articulated, in the back of our minds. We visit them occasionally: they are the stuff of daydreams. We do not give in to them because we are afraid we will fail

Then we must for a moment imagine how we will feel if we do not achieve it. I would not ask you to dwell too long on the negative feelings that come with this, but recognise these are feelings you do not wish to have, so focus again on the outcome you want. We must focus on the rewards and move towards them.

We must recognise, without any excuse or self-delusion, that the moment to take action is here and now. I have talked about living in the present moment, about the power of action, beliefs and attitudes, and that is why when you commit passionately to taking action, things happen. Do something positive to get out of your comfort zone and break the habits of a lifetime. The lazy 'do nothing' frame of mind, which has for so many years become your belief system, your pattern of behaviour, needs to be broken.

Have you seen on film a wounded animal in the wild? It is struggling to get to its feet although it is mortally wounded. This is the most basic life force of all: the will to live. It is the strongest instinct in nature, the most powerful: you see the creature doing everything it can to stay alive.

Self-confidence is the first requisite to great undertakings.

Samuel Johnson (1709–1784)

If your challenge or your goal is simply to overcome shyness or give up smoking, to travel more or to start your own business, you may think it is not a matter of life or death. I think it is certainly a matter of life. Live your dream and you will have the life that you wish for. If you do not take action then the death of your dream is certain. You will have settled for second best, and you will have to live with that knowledge.

> Once your goal is clearly identified, visualise the rewards it will bring. Focus on the positive feelings it will evoke. Think of the personal satisfaction that achieving it will give you. Then harness all of these to fuel your motivation

Just Start As Soon As You Can

As children we are blank sheets of paper; our thoughts and beliefs do not exist in any strong form until our environment and the people around us shape them. Can you remember someone as a child who used to encourage you, who made you feel special? In the absence of a person like that in our adult lives, we must do it for ourselves. We were never taught to be successful, or to be happy. We were brought up to assume that those things just happened if we did our best. You can learn to be successful and learn to be happy, but without the application of motivation that gives rise to positive action, it becomes a very difficult task indeed. Throughout our lives we were taught many things, but sadly we were never taught how to motivate ourselves.

There is no secret technique to motivating yourself. The more powerfully you can create desire, the more likely you are to take action and when the desire feels fit to burst within you, then the motivation will be equally powerful. In Scotland every year on the nearest Saturday to the longest day in the year, the Caledonian

Challenge takes place, a sponsored walk from Fort William, near the foot of Ben Nevis, to Ardlui, on the banks of Loch Lomond. The route is fifty-six miles, north to south, to be completed non-stop. Over 1,200 people enter it every year, and curiously every year the same percentage of the total entrants drop out. Some people have genuine injury-related reasons for dropping out, but the majority of people who do so simply give in. It's understandable: they were very tired, so they quit. Then there are others who finish equally exhausted, who hobble along in obvious discomfort and pain, who walk slowly leaning on their sticks, who can take up to twenty-eight hours. They walk through the night, and through the rain, the hardship and the pain, simply refusing to give up. Motivation will get you to do those things you may naturally not want to do, because you see the greater benefit and understand what has to be done to achieve the goal. Those walkers who are capable of continuing but give up invariably regret it. Many of them come back the following year to complete the walk.

Motivate yourself by living life to the full. It is a long-distance event: never give up, stay focused on your goal, and always look forwards. At the end you will be able to look back and have no regrets. And that is a great goal to have

LIGHT YOUR FIRE

A good way to get motivated is to commit to someone else: to make a promise to achieve a goal. How many people have entered a marathon to raise money for a charity, trained hard and done their best, motivated by the knowledge that their success in finishing the race would benefit others? So when you seek a goal, look for a buddy or someone to actively encourage you and to whom you are accountable. Look to people who have achieved what it is you are trying to do, talk to them, write to them, send them an email, ask them for the motivation that helped them go forward through the hardship. Ask them for their thoughts. You will be amazed how many people will reply. They will share their knowledge and experience. Asking a person who has experience will not only give you the knowledge, but it will inspire you.

> Your motivation is not measured by what you say, but by what you do

Motivation is a fire that needs tending. You must revisit your goal, every day, twice a day if need be and see it clearly in your mind. Fill your mind with positive thoughts, with stories of inspiration. Read books about your heroes. Understand what drove them forward. Understand that your belief in yourself and your ability to succeed will build your confidence step-by-step, stage-by-stage and in so doing will help you build your motivation, and help maintain it.

Identify what lies behind your goal and that will be at the source of your motivation. Motivation is essential to growth and progress. It is not a one-size-fits-all quality – what motivates you may de-motivate someone else. So take time and care to identify what motivates you and then focus on it intently: fill your mind with it every day.

REMEMBER

- No one can motivate you. They can encourage, threaten, inspire or force you. But until you have an overwhelming desire to act then your motivation will be silent
- Once you discover your purpose and passion – you will find your motivation
- True motivation is not theoretical or about knowing. It is about action based on desire and determination

CHAPTER 14

HAPPINESS

Aristotle, the Greek philosopher who lived around 2,300 years ago, concluded after much thought and deliberation that all men and women seek happiness. Though happiness lies beyond acquisition of possessions and power, he believed it gave meaning and purpose to existence. Happiness is simply a state of mind. It is not a random act of chance or good fortune. We are familiar with some of the children of the super-wealthy or those born into royalty, who live miserable, unfulfilled lives.

Happiness is not formulaic, it does not come out of a book or a bottle. It does not get given to us from without, it comes fundamentally from within. It is an individual experience and can be developed by cultivating our perception of experience. Viktor Frankl, the Austrian psychologist and Second World War Holocaust survivor, wrote, 'Success like happiness cannot be pursued, it must ensue'.

Success and happiness occur as a consequence of achieving goals or of experiences we have. You cannot simply be happy by saying to yourself, 'be happy', any more than you can be motivated by saying, 'be motivated'. You have to have something that stimulates both those responses.

Psychologists, who take an independent scientific approach to such matters, look for facts, not abstract notions of religion, faith, or belief, and they have concluded that happiness and success are achieved by controlling the content of our conscious mind. It is further proof that it is not what you do, but how you think that affects the experiences you have along the way.

Action does not always bring happiness; but there is no happiness without action.

Benjamin Disraeli (1804–1881)

Our perception of ourselves and our experiences will derive from conscious choices. How we choose to interpret them is going to be the lasting memory. And from our memories we draw our expectations of the future that will greatly shape the way we think and our attitudes.

Have you ever felt time drag, when the second hand of the clock seems to turn in slow motion? You are trapped in an experience that you cannot wait to finish. Time starts to move so slowly it almost stands still. Maybe you are having a painful dental treatment, or are cornered at a drinks party by a very boring person, who is telling you with great enthusiasm of how they managed to wallpaper their kitchen ceiling. Perhaps it is a sleepless night in a hotel when you have an important meeting in the morning, and you look once again at the clock to discover it is not four hours that have past but simply ten minutes. Or have you ever been aware of the drip, drip of a faulty tap. At those moments we are fully conscious of external events and indeed we are fully aware of our feelings. Generally these will be negative feelings. All our attention is outside us and we are focusing on things over which we have little or no control. When these moments in our lives occur, what words would you use to describe them – boring, tedious, miserable? At that moment, you have become aware of how you feel and you are feeling anything but happy. We become conscious of every passing second.

By contrast we have all experienced moments in our life, and I hope we continue to experience them, which are quite simply timeless. It is as though time has stood still. These moments are almost never passive, and they are rarely random. They are moments when we are fully engaged in the moment.

> Happiness is a state of mind, an experience of the here and now, so don't make it conditional on future events. Like love, make happiness unconditional

IN THE ZONE

In the world of professional and amateur sport when people perform at a level often beyond anything they have done before: they are fully engaged in the moment with no room for nerves – they have gone beyond conscious thought. This state is often referred to as 'being in the zone'. It is as though they are on autopilot. They have transcended thought and feeling and are in a total state of 'being'. People talk of being unaware of the outside world around them. It is not only champion athletes. We can find these moments in our own lives. Have you ever spoken with a stranger you meet on a flight or at a social event who tells you a moving story and you are completely transfixed by it, engrossed in the emotion of the moment. When you realise you are so engrossed you are unaware of your surroundings.

Simple events can create this feeling of peace, of oneness. They are positive emotions, positive feelings and positive thoughts. Psychologists have a term for this; they call it optimum experience or flow. It is when you are so involved in an activity that nothing else seems to matter. Have you ever seen a child in a sandpit building a sandcastle? You call their name; they do not hear you because they are completely and utterly engrossed in the moment.

Pelé, the great Brazilian footballer, described it as a strange calmness, a feeling that he only experienced in football, a type of euphoria, in which he could run without tiring, he could make the ball do whatever he wanted, with a feeling that whatever happened he would not be hurt.

Most folks are about as happy as they make up their minds to be.

Abraham Lincoln (1809–1865)

These moments of timeless experience come, I believe, when we let go of conscious thought and in the moment allow our subconscious mind to fully engage our bodies. Many athletes performing at the peak of their ability, when asked what they were thinking about during the game, unsurprisingly say that they thought of nothing at all. We can trust our subconscious mind to enable us to engage in what it is we want to do. It puts us in autopilot, where we will find the ability to commit to repetitive tasks that need to be done, and though we may be aware of time, it is no longer our enemy. Boredom, fatigue and distress are less likely to be present when we are engaged in the moment and perform at our best. In an earlier chapter I talked about the importance of here and now, of living in the present moment. Research indicates that when you can engage fully in your activity in the present you create for yourself maximum opportunity to succeed.

SPONTANEOUS HAPPINESS

Have you ever gone out with some friends for an informal pizza and a beer? You meet up as arranged and have a few drinks and some food to eat, and then you start to reminisce and tell each other stories. You talk about what is going on now. You tell each other jokes. Laughter is flowing. It is heartfelt laughter that comes from deep within. We are thoroughly enjoying the moment, we laugh and enjoy, feel oneness with our friends. It is a magical night, a night that is burned so deeply into our minds that we will remember it for a long time. Whenever we recall it, we will have that wonderful feeling. We want it to just go on forever.

Happiness is inward, and not outward; and so, it does not depend on what we have, but on what we are.

Henry Van Dyke, American clergyman and writer
(1852–1933)

The key to mastery of one's life is through control of our conscious mind, through using it to influence our subconscious mind. There are two schools of thought about life, the religious or spiritual view, and the scientific or secular view. People on different sides will tell the other they are wrong, that they have erroneous beliefs which will misguide them. But it does not matter what you believe, as long as you believe above all in yourself and your ability to be successful and happy.

> You could spend the rest of your life reading books on philosophy and psychology and still be less sure about happiness than if you gave time to defining for yourself what it is you want out of life

THE FOUR TRAITS COMMON TO HAPPY PEOPLE

Research into happiness has identified some common traits. The first, is that happy people are positive. They tend to be optimistic, to have a positive outlook and a positive attitude. They tend to succeed more in life. They have, unsurprisingly, better immune systems and recover from ill health more quickly.

The second trait is that they have good self-esteem. This means they like themselves, despite whatever shortcomings they may have, or their physical appearance: they feel good about themselves. They are not delusional and do not hide behind masks and status symbols, they simply accept themselves as they are. They are realistic.

The third trait is they have control. They believe they have control of their destinies. Surveys show that people who feel in control tend to have more feelings of happiness in their lives. They are more goal-orientated as a result. They achieve more at school, cope better in life, suffer less stress, and consider themselves to be happy.

The fourth quality is that they tend to be outgoing. Happy people tend to be not big extroverts, but friendly and open. They tend to interact with social groups well, and have circles of friends with whom they mingle on a regular basis. They engage in rewarding social and personal activities. They give and experience more affection in life.

Happy people act happy, they manage their time, they engage with their skills, they do things they enjoy, they savour the moment, and they live in the present.

Now and then it's good to pause in our pursuit of happiness and just be happy.

Guillaume Apollinaire, French poet (1880-1918)

A Smile Is A Smile, Or Is It?

When someone smiles we will normally assume that they are happy. Or are they? Have you ever been asked to smile for the camera when you quite frankly were not in the mood and were having a bit of a bad hair day? I came across a very fascinating piece of research on smiling that was conducted over a 25-year period. There are two types of smile. One is known as the Duchenne smile, named after its discoverer Guillaume Duchenne. The researcher identified this smile, which was different from the average smile. He noticed that when a smile is spontaneous, radiant, joyful and comes from within, it is a direct response to true feelings of happiness. The corner of the mouth turns up and the eyes crinkle up. The muscles which accomplish this crinkling around the eye are very hard to control voluntarily. The other smile is the forced or unnatural smile, which often people plaster on their face when they are told to smile. The researchers refer to this as the Pan American smile, named after the airline, Pan American Airways as its air hostesses had what they considered to be a sort of cheesy fake grin. The article indicated that trained psychologists could differentiate from a photograph between the two smiles. So therefore by looking at the photograph, looking at the position of the corners of the mouth, and the amount of crinkling around the eyes they can tell a real smile based on true happiness and inner joy, from a fake smile based on just grinning inanely.

A happy smile from the heart costs nothing, yet the joy it can spread is priceless

The researchers decided that they would look through a collection of photographs taken in the past and separate out what they believed was the genuinely happy smile from the artificial smile. The two researchers from the University of California in Berkeley studied photographs from a 1960 yearbook from Mills College, in which there were 141 senior class photographs. All but three of the women in the photographs were smiling. Half of the smiles were identified as being authentic joyful smiles, and the others artificial. All of the women in the photograph were contacted at the age of twenty-seven, then again at forty-three and fifty-two. They were asked questions about their life satisfaction, their experiences and their happiness.

The researchers had wondered, based on the type of smiles in the photographs taken in 1960, whether it would be possible to predict who would have happy fulfilling lives and who would not. Astonishingly the results turned out that those who were authentically happy or demonstrated the Duchenne smile were on average more likely to be married, more likely to stay married and more likely to experience personal well-being over the 30-year period. Those indicators were predicted merely by the position of the crinkles around their eyes, by those muscles, which cannot be voluntarily moved.

The researchers asked if was there anything else differentiating these women? For example, did they come from wealthier families, did they have more privileges, were they simply much more attractive and therefore likely to find more secure partners? The researchers went back and rated these qualities. They discovered that how the women looked had nothing to do with the quality and longevity of their marriages, and their sense of life satisfaction. So the research concluded that those smiling, happy women genuinely turned out happy in life. Are there any major surprises there? A real smile is different from a forced one. Many people say they feel happier when they have done something spontaneously kind and helpful to another person, than when they have participated in a planned activity.

You just have to know what it means to be happy.

IS SUCCESS AN END IN ITSELF?

Behind every goal lies a purpose. Purpose creates our feelings of well-being and success. Is there anything beyond success? Do we get to a point in our lives having achieved all the goals we set out to achieve, when we can realistically think there is no more? Acquisition of property, power, wealth, status, loving relationships is fine, and for many people that is enough. But I think beyond success lies meaning and purpose – a personal sense of significance. That sense is a measure of our contribution to life, to the world at large, through the actions we take to benefit other people.

Many people have told me that their greatest success was when they did something for someone else. Often these were random acts of kindness. We enter this world with nothing and we leave it the same way. What we achieve beyond material rewards in life is in the service of our fellow man, and in doing that we create lasting value. We are not the centre of the universe, we are simply a part of it. Our ability to play our part will give us all a sense of meaning and purpose.

> The most important thing is that whatever you believe, it should enable you to live your life positively and to create true happiness for yourself

Inasmuch as we can help others in simple ways, we are also helping ourselves to grow emotionally and spiritually. You need to find your own sense of purpose. There is not a one-size-fits all: for those who are spiritual, their meaning and purpose may be obvious, while those who believe in the scientific and rational, will also discover their purpose and meaning. It is not important that we all share the same purpose and meaning. To know that the actions you take will positively impact on another person, to have given freely to another without need of reward, praise or power, I believe is of the highest value.

HAPPINESS IS WITHIN US

Let me return for a moment to an earlier theme that is related to our happiness. If our lives are journeys of discovery, exactly what is it that we are meant to discover? Aristotle believed it was happiness. Other philosophers will tell you it is a personal sense of meaning out of random existence; spiritual teachers will tell you it is the discovery of our souls and our oneness with God; scientists will tell you, it is the popular theory of the moment or maybe nothing at all. No one can answer the question for you. But if you look within, you will find sufficient understanding. When you start to meditate to still your mind and go to deeper levels of consciousness, you will experience a sense of peace and oneness. What name you give it is up to you. It may be just peace and serenity. Some may explain it as a psychological phenomenon, others as a spiritual experience. It does not matter, if it fits in with your beliefs that is fine. Take advantage of the opportunity such reflection provides you with.

> Happiness is a conscious choice

While the great religious teachers seem to have a great deal in common with shared ethical and moral codes, love, and respect of life, which we sometimes find too difficult to live up to, we must accept people as they are, not as we want them to be. We must not be judgemental; we must do our best in helping others to grow. We feel more in touch with others when we do so.

So, what is your aspiration for your life? You should think about it. It does not need to involve philosophical pondering on the deep questions of life such as who am I and why am I here? Many of us have spent long anxious nights in a sort of existential quandary, trying to figure it out, and there are more books written on this topic than you could hope to read in one lifetime. History records some religions and beliefs as they come and they go, but they only help to make sense of the world as it was at that time. The only world that you can make sense of is your world, and that is why you should spend time thinking about what lies beyond success.

We act as though comfort and luxury are the chief requirements of life, when all we need to be happy is something to be enthusiastic about.

Charles Kingsley, clergyman and novelist (1819–1875)

I know that at the times when we disengage the conscious mind, and live in the moment, we experience happiness and timelessness. Look at young children playing, squealing with delight at the simplest of pleasures, running through a puddle or playing chase. They are fully alive in the present, the now. Their happiness is not conditional on understanding or intellectual reasoning, they have not studied philosophy or religion, they have not got themselves involved in anything other than the moment. They live in and for the present and we can glimpse their joy. I feel that within each and every one of us, the possibility to experience such joy exists. It's not complicated or difficult. Unclutter your life. Don't ask what makes you happy.

Just do the things you love and you will find happiness there.

REMEMBER

- Happiness is a state of mind, it is a conscious choice
- Like love, true happiness is unconditional, it is a feeling of the moment based on how we feel
- Happy people are positive, have high self-esteem, believe they are in control of their future, and are friendly and open. All are traits we can aquire

CHAPTER 15

YOU
ABSOLUTELY
NEED A PLAN

Whatever goal you set yourself, no matter how much visualisation you do, no matter how committed you are to it, no matter how much will-power and enthusiasm you can demonstrate, until you take action nothing is going to happen. And to take the right action requires focused and detailed planning.

The focus for the action will be found in the creation of a strategy or a plan. First, you clearly identify your goal, what it is you want to do. Second, you create a realistic timeframe for doing it. Only then can you work on the actual plan that will enable you to realise the goal. Strong self-belief, confidence, commitment, determination are all wonderful qualities but they need to be focused towards the goal, by using a plan that is easy to follow and implement.

Major life goals often overwhelm people, even though they are realistic – the size and scale can seem insurmountable to us. When you look at the challenges involved, you find it difficult to break them down into smaller sub-goals, milestones to measure your progress

Many people mistakenly think they will achieve their goals through the sheer power of determination and desire. They run out enthusiastically and set about being very busy and very active. They are working hard but they are not necessarily working smart. To work smart, you need to work towards your goals by taking active steps that move you forward. The action plan becomes a road map. It is your way of measuring time and distance and direction to your goal. Once you clearly identify your goal and the time in which you wish it to happen, you will naturally start to work on the 'how', and the 'how' is the starting point for your plan.

As mentioned before, behind our goals lies purpose. We said the achievement of a goal gives us something. It may give us freedom, piece of mind, financial security, but generally speaking the goal enables us to fulfil a purpose.

A plan is only a plan – like a recipe in a cookery book, until commitment to action is taken nothing happens

We live our lives moving forward, though it may feel sometimes like it is going backwards when we have particularly frustrating experiences. We must look forward to the goals we have set, and we must create a map and a compass to help us get there. No matter how large your goal may be you must break them down into small more manageable steps. Just as the sculptor creates his statue one strike of the hammer at a time, as the artist paints a picture one brushstroke at a time, and the writer creates a book one word at a time, we must check each detail.

In today's fast-pace society, people want things now: they're in a hurry, they don't want to wait and take the time necessary to achieve their goal. But life doesn't work like that. Planning the time frame for your goal gives you an accurate perspective of what needs to be done, in what order and by when. It will prevent you becoming disillusioned and frustrated by any apparent lack of progress

When you arrange to have friends to your house for supper, it is likely you will plan in advance what you want to eat. You will look at some recipe books or maybe some of your own concoctions will be the dish of the day. Most people will write out a list of the ingredients to buy. They will go to the store ticking off each ingredient from the list. The hour people will be eating is factored in to allow the food to be prepared in the right order so it will be ready at the right time. You put your wine in the fridge, have a good supply of water, you lay the table and work out in advance where you want people to sit. One of your recipes may be slightly new to you or complicated, so you read a recipe book. And that is all a plan is. It is a logical sequence of instructions you give yourself that you can measure your progress through.

The majority of men meet with failure because of their lack of persistence in creating new plans to take the place of those which fail.

Napoleon Hill, writer (1883–1970)

DO NOT LEAVE YOUR LIFE TO CHANCE

When I started my business many years ago, the first course I offered was team building. I would set up day-long events where people could learn new skills and then at the end of the day be given a great challenge where they could put together everything they had learned that day in a sequential order to compete against other teams, the clock and most of all themselves. I noted with interest over the many courses I ran, that some teams who won were energetic, enthusiastic and could not wait to get started, while other winning teams seemed reserved, and quiet. At first I was not able to predict which would be the winning team, but I soon learned that the team who spent the most time planning every stage of the event was inevitably the one that ran into the fewest problems, and almost always won.

They would examine the problem and be very clear about the challenge it faced them with. They would understand exactly what the goal was, then they would then break it down to smaller and smaller parts, allocate tasks to individuals or groups within their team and collectively work together. They would be a much more powerful force than the others who would quickly read the challenge and then run off without explaining to others what they were doing or approach the problem from the wrong end. Having a plan or a strategy is absolutely vital in achieving your goals in life.

SIMPLICITY IS THE KEY

I am not a fan of complexity. Life is simple. We can add layer upon layer to it, to give it more depth and a feeling of texture but if we strip it down to the bare bones, we will inevitably find that there are simple principles involved.

There are seven steps to creating a plan.

First, clearly identify the goal so that you are in absolutely no doubt as to what you are seeking to achieve, understand what it looks like, indeed what it feels like.

Second, write down a completion date when you want this goal to be achieved.

Third, identify the stages between starting and completion. Write these stages down as objectives or mini-goals that need to be completed and choose a date or anticipated length of time that they will take.

Fourth, identify the challenges or the lack of knowledge you currently have and then create solutions for the challenges or acquire the knowledge you need.

Fifth, create a reward for achieving each of the mini-goals. These rewards can be simple, or extravagant. They help to reinforce a stronger self-image of success and personal achievement in the subconscious mind.

Sixth, revisit your goal and your plan on a daily basis. You must be able to see your progress on a day-to-day basis or identify actions you have to take.

Seven, adjust the timeframe or the plan as necessary but continue to move towards your goal.

Those seven steps are all you need to have an effective strategy for your life.

Simplicity in character, in manners, in style; in all things the supreme excellence is simplicity.

Henry Wadsworth Longfellow, poet (1807–1882)

YOUR FLIGHT PLAN FOR LIFE

In the world of business a great deal of time is put into project management, strategic planning and forward development of the business. Jobs and cash flow depends on planning, they cannot be left to chance. We too need to create for ourselves our own form of project management and forward planning. If your plans are vague, fuzzy and unstructured, so too will your results be. We must not bumble along through life, hoping that things will work out; your life is full of opportunities if you just seek them.

When you take a flight en route to your holiday destination, you proceed through a routine series of actions. You travel to the airport, you check in, and once your flight is called you board the aircraft. You sit down in your pre-assigned seat, and hopefully there you can relax. You are confident that the pilots know where they are going, have plotted their course, the flight duration and the distance, made all the relevant checks and understand what they are doing. Let us apply the seven stages of planning to the flight.

The first step is to clearly identify the goal. The destination of the flight.

The second step is to write down a completion date. Estimate the arrival time.

The third step, identify the stages and the points in your timeline and the small goals you have to achieve. In aviation, the pilot plots an exact route, with waypoints along the way to measure time and distance.

The fourth step, identify challenges and create solutions. Before they take off the pilots have a weather check on the route so they can avoid bad weather. They will also be aware of the position of other aircraft as they fly through the route and adjust their route accordingly.

The fifth step; create a reward for achieving successful mini-goals along the way. Well I guess this is where we may deviate. I don't imagine the pilot and co-pilot are having a party in the cockpit every time they pass a waypoint but I do hope they take some professional pride in being on time, on target and doing it safely. Getting to the destination and through all points safely is their reward.

The sixth, revisit your goals regularly. The pilots will regularly check their time, their position and their direction. They keep an eye on the instrument panel and the route indicator.

The seventh step, is adjust your timeframe or plan if required. If bad weather ensues or there are any engine problems, the pilots will accordingly adjust their destination if need be. Flights have turned back or landed at other airports when necessary.

> All the principles behind success are simple. When we create our plan for the grand goal of life it may look overwhelming to us – but if we break it down into small manageable goals you will find it really is simple

ONE STEP AT A TIME

Imagine wanting to walk around the world. A British man, Karl Bushby plans to do exactly that. In November 1998 he set off from Tierra del Fuego, the most southern point in South America, with the intention of walking 36,000 miles around the world. His timeframe is ten years. On his website he says, 'We all live with dreams, set our own goals, make choices and ultimately decisions'.

In May 2004, six years after he began, Karl had reached Fairbanks Alaska, and had covered 15,000 miles. He will soon finalise plans to cross the ice of the Baring Strait in the spring.

Ultimately decisions have to be taken and these decisions come down to this: take action or do not take action. But without a plan taking action at best will be a haphazard event.

We have too many high-sounding words, and too few actions that correspond with them.

Abigail Adams, American writer and early feminist
(1744–1818)

Another quotation from Karl Bushby, 'As regards planning: simplicity and flexibility are the foundations upon which this expedition are built'. So here is my million-dollar question for you: for all the goal-setting, planning, commitment, determination, focus, enthusiasm and motivation, how exactly is Karl going to achieve his goal? The answer is one step at a time – and so it is with our plans. We must make them manageable. We must know the next step we need to take, and we must not worry that this step is in the wrong direction because we will discover soon enough if it is not working. The plan is the map you can return to, to measure your time, your distance, your progress and your direction. If your plan is not working, change it.

You can gain knowledge, find information, you can go back to college, read books, and ask others for their advice. Someone will always be able to help you. If you need advice ask, get a mentor or write to people who have achieved what you are trying to achieve. But whatever you do, begin planning, and when the plan is in place; you must take action.

The time you have is a precious commodity. The reality is you do not possess time. Time passes and once gone we never get it back. Concentrate on what your goal is, and, then set a timeframe for achieving it

WRITE YOUR LIFE GOALS

As soon as you have identified your goal and created your plan, start. Start now. Write down a list of fifty things you want to do in the next ten years – they can be small goals, they can be grand goals – and then begin writing a plan. Break your goals down into small manageable steps. I recommend you write down daily actions to be taken, step-by-step, until you get there. Planning can be as simple and reactive as you want it to be, or as detailed and complex as you need. There is no one way to create a plan. All you need to do is have a good sense of how.

The pyramids in Egypt are one of the wonders of the world. They are a staggering feat of precision engineering that took thirty years to build by the human sweat of more than 5,000 people. The engineers and the architects knew exactly what they were doing. The stones were cut to exact precision, placed in an exact order, and they created a building, which even now can take your breath away. The pyramids were planned. So are most of the great achievements in life.

A flexible plan is one of the principles of success. Without planning we have randomness and chaos. Something will result from unplanned actions because it always does, but the odds of it being exactly what you want to happen are unlikely. When you visualise your goal your subconscious mind will be working towards it. When you add a plan, your subconscious mind will absorb that plan and look for opportunities. That is why coincidence and opportunity become much more prevalent in your life.

Your plan will be a road map to your goals, and if it is not working, you should change it. You can always change the plan – it is the goal that should always remain the same.

REMEMBER

- A plan well made is like a route map, it will let you know where you are, and how far you have to go
- Keep your plans simple, and broken down into small manageable steps
- If your plan isn't working – change it!

CHAPTER 16

YOUR LIFE

Your life is here and now, and it is for living. Your ability to create the success you want in life, and have the life you seek, is up to you. No one is going to do it for you, but the good news is you really can do it.

When you lift an arm, open a door, or jump for joy, all those physical actions are initiated by will-power. It is will-power that starts the whole process. Without will-power nothing is going to happen. We often mistake power for being something dramatic. The true power that you need to get started and on the road to success is within you. Remember your life is your responsibility, so accept that responsibility and continue to strive for your goals. Do not give in. If you develop the habit of giving in every time the going gets tough you will lose your will-power.

> Recognise that you are in control of your actions. So by accepting responsibility and taking the right actions we can create our life goals

Some people tell you that they just do not have the will-power to follow through on the things in their life that they want to change. Who do they imagine is responsible for their will-power?

The way they think, what they believe and their will-power are all their responsibility, and they have chosen not to accept it. They have absolved themselves of the consequences of their actions because 'it's not their fault, it's just the way it is'. Those people are wrong.

> Use what talents you possess: the woods would be very silent if no birds sang there except those that sang best.
>
> *Henry Van Dyke* (1852–1933)

When you hear of someone who gets up at 5.30 in the morning to go to the gym or go for a run, what is your reaction? Do you think they're mad? Or do you have a quiet admiration for their ability to commit to a definite plan of action, and just get on and do it. I think we admire and respect them because they have will-power, and choose to use it to make positive change.

NEVER SAY DIE

The American cyclist Lance Armstrong has won the Tour de France, the most gruelling bicycle race in the world, for an incredible six consecutive years. The race covers over 3,300 kilometres in a three-week period. Lance Armstrong famously overcame cancer, but while in hospital he was dropped by the French team that sponsored him. The US Postal team signed him up to ride for them and gave him a new sponsorship deal. In 1999, three years after having been given a 40 per cent chance of recovery from a cancer that had spread to his lungs and brain, he won the Tour de France, and went on to win it five successive times, with a record-breaking sixth consecutive victory in July 2004.

At a time in professional cycling when some top riders were being found guilty of using performance-enhancing drugs, Lance Armstrong was frequently tested at random. He was always clean. People could not believe how this man, a cancer survivor, had not only won the Tour de France, but continued to dominate the event. He had not used any drugs of any kind. One sensed in fact there was disappointment in certain camps that he could not be found to be using any artificial stimulants to improve his performance. During one interview a journalist asked him, what he was on. Lance Armstrong said, 'I'll tell you what I'm on, I'm on my ass in the saddle six hours a day practising as hard as I can'.

What Lance Armstrong has is what all peak performers have and all champions have: they have the will to win. Do you?

THE TOP THREE INCHES

There was an old rugby coach, who when getting his players ready for the match immediately before kick off, would gather the team around him. He wanted the team to have the right mind-set as they ran out, but he did not try rabble-rousing motivational slogans to get them going, nor did he point to his heart in any emotional or patriotic gestures. Instead he would point to the top of his head and say, 'Remember the top three inches'. What he meant was, the will to win is in your mind. Your will-power exists in your mind and you can access it any time you want to. It will take you anywhere you want to go. Your conscious mind is under your control – all you have to do is engage it.

Many people are born with remarkable talents and abilities, and yet they achieve nothing in life except regret for what they failed to do. And there are others of more average ability, who somehow reached the dizzy heights of success. What separated them? The answer is simple: the will to win

People who have a negative belief in themselves and negative attitudes, can also develop will-power, but it will be manifested in a negative way. They will be stubborn. They are the very people who will 'cut off their nose to spite their face'. They will deny themselves pleasure and make other people feel bad. Put negative beliefs and attitudes behind your will and you create a negative outcome; put positive attitude behind it and you can create magic. How you direct your will is up to you.

As is our confidence, so is our capacity.

William Hazlitt, English essayist and critic (1778–1830)

Philosophers and religious writers refer to this unique human quality that we all possess as free will. Choose to use it. Two people can be born at the same time, in the same area, with the same opportunities but they live two very different lives. Much of it is to do with expectation and desire, and yet you will find the one who got to the top will have demonstrated all the qualities that we have discussed in this book, and a will to win.

If you make no effort to engage your will-power, you will become easily distracted and you will go off course. Your plans will go awry, your determination will falter, and you will justify your actions with all the excuses in the world. This does not make you a bad person, it just simply stops you from progressing towards your goal, so recognise that you really do have the power within you. Repeated failures may have allowed you to convince yourself that you cannot succeed. You can.

DO NOT BE AFRAID

I can think of few more encouraging words in the world than a sincere, 'Don't be afraid'. If you were to ask me for one crucial piece of advice it would be just that – 'don't be afraid'. If you can find the courage to reach beyond your current level of expectation you will grow.

> We can waste our whole lives worrying about things that never happen, excusing ourselves and spending needless energy on finding reasons not to do what we really want to do

In your own life, look back at the successes you achieved. Can you remember someone who encouraged you at that point, a teacher, a parent or a friend? Can you remember standing on the high board at the swimming pool, a friend who believed in you looking up and saying, 'Do it, you can do it', and encouraging you to believe. They were not shouting, 'Don't do it, you'll get hurt'. They encouraged you then but they may not be here now. In the absence of such a person – you must learn to encourage yourself. You can do it, if you really believe you can.

All our dreams can come true, if we have the courage to pursue them.

Walt Disney (1901–1966)

A girl told me that her life changed after I had told her that I thought she was talented, and should consider going to college, and that I invited her to my office to explore career options. I had not even remembered having that conversation, but she told me nine years later, that no one had ever believed in her before and made her really believe that she could succeed. She told me that she stayed at school for an extra year, and went to college where she studied marketing and business studies. When I met her nine years later it was at a conference for a large international company, where she now held a senior position in the marketing department.

In the absence of somebody to encourage you, encourage yourself.

REMEMBER

- No matter what you might believe – *you are* in control of your life
- Imagine how you will want to be remembered, and then go out and make your dreams a reality
- Every day is a new opportunity, when you have goals for the future, you will start to see them
- This is your life – live it to the full

PART 3

THINGS YOU
NEED TO DO

 You are unique

How To Use
Part 3

The following exercises will enable you to achieve your goals. If you want to go through them in one go that is fine, but without repeated daily application nothing will happen. The lessons are to give you an opportunity to recap on much of what has been examined in greater detail earlier in the book, but also to help you reflect on where you are and how to proceed from here. You can re-visit any section as a refresher whenever to want to, but once you get it, you will have it for the rest of your life. These are the tools you will be able to use any time and anywhere.

Within a short time you should be using the visualisation process to achieve all the changes in your life that you want to. Everything you dream of achieving is possible. If it can be visualised and within the realms of the possible, then it can be accomplished.

There are eight exercises to be performed as required, after one has completed the visualisation process. A good way to think of it is the visualisation process is rather like the gym – it is the place where you are able to do the exercises to maximum benefit. Just as the gym allows you to access the equipment you need to get fit, so too the visualisation process allows you to access the mental exercises that will enable you to change your life.

THE EXERCISES

The exercises are short and simple, easy to understand and to incorporate into your life. In Part 2 you will have gained an insight of the emotions, factors and dynamics that are central to our growth and success.

I have talked repeatedly about the importance of having a plan and taking action, but if we truly want to change we must see ourselves as changing, and see ourselves as being successful. Therefore at the heart of this series of lessons and exercises is the core concept of actually being able to 'see' the changes in your mind. Just like physical exercise programmes these exercises only work when you apply them directly. At the very heart of this process of changing your life is self-guided visualisation.

I will take you through the visualisation procedure I use, to get to the deeper levels. It will take practice and may, in the very early days, feel as though nothing is happening – it is. Every time you visualise, you will improve your effectiveness. For a while progress may be slow and you may not feel you are in the deep state for a long time but it will come – stick with it. It took me about six weeks of trying twice day before I was aware of it all just clicking into place. If I can do it, you can too.

I have studied meditation and visualisation, and borrowed from my father's hypnotic techniques of auto-suggestion. In the process I have developed a method that works for me and is simple and easy to use. If you already use other meditation and visualisation methods, then by all means stick with what is most comfortable for you. The important thing is that you can get into a relaxed state where you can change your beliefs.

The challenge of meditation is that we have to still our minds. Once we have done this, we have to activate it again to re-programme new beliefs and attitudes into our brain through visualisations. For some people this seems difficult – how can you still your mind and then make it active again and remain calm? In fact when we still our minds through conscious relaxation, our brain cycle slows down and we go into the alpha state. In the alpha state we are able to actively programme our mind without too much distraction. In the very early stages you may find that you are easily distracted, or that you end up daydreaming. Do not worry. These are all natural occurrences – your brain has been busy all your life, and is unused to being still, now that you are consciously trying to still it. As with all techniques it becomes faster, easier and more efficient with time. Eventually you will get to the deep alpha state very quickly and there will be no random thoughts to distract you.

The exercises will involve visualisation where you will actually replace limiting beliefs, attitudes, poor self-image and really 'see' yourself, having successfully changed.

So please don't give up on this journey of a lifetime. Stick with it. Your ability to change your life is found in your mind, when you change your thoughts and beliefs about yourself and your future, then the behaviours will follow. Some people go deep first time, others, like me, can take a while – but remember you will get out what you put in, so be sure to put the time in. So take your time to learn the visualisation technique and by following the eight exercises you will begin the journey of a lifetime.

The
Visualisation
Technique

Sit down in a chair with your legs uncrossed, keeping your back reasonably upright, it is important that you do not slouch, or get into a position in which you can fall asleep. The important thing is to sit in a relaxed manner. Your feet should be both planted on the floor, your hands may be gently resting on top of your legs or gently clasped together, at this point,

Begin to consciously breathe in deeply, and slowly breathe out, deeply and slowly. And as you breathe in, say to yourself a positive affirmation, feel the associated emotions and positive thoughts coming into your body renewing you, energising you, making you stronger and immediately becoming part of you. As you breathe out, be aware of the new positive thoughts replacing the negative thoughts which are now leaving your body. For example:

I am breathing in health.............I am breathing out sickness

I am breathing in courage ....I am breathing out fear

I am breathing in joy ....I am breathing out sadness

I am breathing in love........................I am breathing out hate

I am breathing in light...............I am breathing out darkness

I am breathing in fun ....I am breathing out frustration

I am breathing in calm ....I am breathing out tension

I am breathing in peace ....I am breathing out anxiety

Identify and choose positive emotions that you wish to feel in your life, and breathe out the negative emotions you want to release. As you do this, imagine the air entering your body, imagine the good going in and the negative going out.

After ten or twelve deep breaths just simply focus on your breathing and breathe in, breathe out. As you breathe in, consciously relax your body. Breathe in for the first part, then out for the remainder of the statement:

My legs are relaxing ....they are relaxed

My abdomen is relaxing ....my abdomen is relaxed

The muscles in my back are relaxing...........they are relaxed

The muscles in my neck are relaxing...........they are relaxed

My arms are relaxing ....they are relaxed

My chest muscles are relaxing.....................they are relaxed

My facial muscles are relaxing.....................they are relaxed

This is you consciously instructing the muscles in your body to become more relaxed. As you physically become more relaxed, your mental state will follow. Your physiological and mental states are very closely related.

In this relaxed physical state concentrate as you breathe in and out. You have relaxed the muscle groups, at this point move into a deeper conscious state of meditation by counting slowly from ten back to one.

As you do so tell yourself you are going into deeper relaxation. For example:

Ten: I am moving to deeper levels of relaxation.

Nine, eight, seven: my mind is growing quieter and quieter.

Six, five, four: moving down to a state of calm and deep relaxation.

Three, two, one: I am now fully and deeply relaxed and quiet.

You are now ready to manage your active visualisation.

I want you to visualise that you are at a place where you are very happy, and feel safe and secure. It can be a real place you have visited in your life, or it can be an imagined place that you have always dreamt of going. The important thing it is a place where you feel happy and relaxed, it can be on a beach, a favourite room, the place is not as important as the feelings it evokes. A feeling of calm security and peacefulness. When you arrive in this place be aware of your surroundings. Look around, what do you see? Listen, what do you hear?

Now, become aware of a set of doors in this scene. Move towards and then walk through them and imagine a corridor formed by people you know, family and friends (even people you don't know personally but simply admire). As you walk down this corridor they are patting you on the back and are pleased to see you, they are smiling at you. As you see them smiling, you feel the warmth of being loved, you feel good about yourself, you feel positive: you're being appreciated, you're motivated, you're feeling full of energy. You feel your self-confidence soar – you feel wonderful.

When you get to the end of the human corridor, walk through two more doors and enter a cinema. Take a seat. As soon as you do, the lights dim and the curtains part. Up on the screen, the words 'Previously Showing' appear. On the screen, project positive memories of success from your life, memories of achievement and happiness, moments when you have felt fully alive, fully successful, proud and happy. Focus on these memories from your past. Then get out of the seat and step into the picture, and once again re-live these moments and feel the emotions that you associate with these experiences. Re-live them and connect with the strong feelings of love and confidence that were present.

Then return to your seat. The screen changes and you see the words, 'Now Showing'. This is your life as it is right now. Look at the aspects of your life you do not like, such as being overweight, in an unfulfilling relationship or in a dead-end job. Look at the aspects of your life that you do not like and then simply freeze that picture. Let it turn to black and white. Do not enter this picture but slowly let it fade away. This screen is where you will project the aspects of your current life that you want to change. It is an important screen because it is where the old habits, attitudes and negative thinking are identified and erased. Therefore when you identify each aspect of your life that you do not like, you will see it in terms of an action. When the action is identified, freeze the picture, turn it to black and white and let it shrink and fade away.

When you have finished removing the negative, have the words, 'Coming Soon' appear on the screen. Now you can start to create your future. Project onto the screen the powerful goals that you have set yourself. If your dream is to stand upon the summit of Mount Everest, see yourself standing there, ice axe in one hand, raised fist in the other, and see yourself smiling. Create a vivid image. Step into that picture and see the 'you in the future' look around from the summit down the mountain below. Look into the eyes of the Sherpa with you on the summit and see the smile and happiness for you in his eyes. You can repeat this for as many future goals as you may have. Project whatever goals you have for yourself onto the screen and become a part of it. You are now making a connection from past successes to future successes. The past successes have happened, and your mind is able to recall the feelings and emotions associated with them. Your mind is now seeing the future successes, and now subconsciously believes that they are going to happen in the future. You should also visualise every other significant goal you need to achieve en route to the desired final outcome. Then continue to focus on the big goals in your life. Project them powerfully and at a moment during that visualisation when you feel fully connected, form a fist, or squeeze a thumb and finger together. This gives you a physical action, a connection to this emotional feeling and future memory.

Return to your seat. When you are ready, get up and leave the cinema. You look around you in the corridor and this time your friends, well wishers, and characters you admire are still there, but they are cheering wildly with love and joy, because they can see you are changing into a new person, they see your future success.

When you leave the cinema, you have returned to the safe and serene place you chose to be (where ever that might be). Now I want you to count from one to ten slowly. If you have difficulty or want to visualise more efficiently and quickly, you can purchase guided visualisation CDs from my website (see Appendix for details). As you do, become more and more aware of returning to being fully awake and aware. At this point you are now moving from the alpha state to the beta state. Continue to come back to full awareness slowly but surely. In your own time, open your eyes.

And that is it. It is not only easy, it gets better and faster. I suggest fifteen minutes morning or evening. I would recommend twice a day but if that is too much then at least once a day minimum. Also, if you have had a stressful day or are going to be very busy in the coming days, you can remain in a state of relaxation by staying in your imagined favourite place for longer after the visualisation exercise and just relax. The health benefits alone are wonderful: reduced heart rate, lowered blood pressure, and a very relaxed physiology.

Exercise 1
Take Stock

We have examined in detail the impact that our attitudes and beliefs have in our lives. They have formed since early childhood – they shape the way we see the world and the world sees us.

Change them and you can change your life.

Before you can change your beliefs and attitudes you need to assess them honestly – a stock check. You need to examine the thinking that you need to change. There is an old saying, 'To change what you get, you must change what you are'.

In this exercise we will look at 'What we are'.

We will identify the current thinking, attitudes and beliefs that we currently have in place. Just like a computer software programme, we will use the information to enable us to replace it with the right thoughts, beliefs, feelings and attitudes. Once you do that, your subconscious mind aligns your behaviour with the new self-image.

- Make a table with three columns – positive, negative and change.

- In the positive column make a list of your positive beliefs, attitudes and aspects of you that you are proud of and that you like.

- In the second column do the same for the negative beliefs, attitudes and aspects of you that prevent you being your best self.

- Make a list in the third column of the opposite qualities that you have listed in the negative column. This is the first part of helping you identify the beliefs you need to adapt to make changes. Remember you are dealing with lifelong conditioning that you currently may believe that you cannot just change. You will be pleasantly surprised to discover that by actively identifying with the new beliefs you need you will be able to incorporate them into your visualisation.

When you finish your table may look something like this.

Positive	Negative	To change negative to positive I must
Enthusiastic	Selfish	Be selfless
Willing to try new things	Feelings of inadequacy	Love self unconditionally
Good job with prospects	Overreact to criticism	Practice calmness in the moment
Good health	Drink too much	Stop drinking
	Feel unattractive	Love self unconditionally
	Anxious most of the time	Practice calmness in the moment
	Hate my boss	Love the person, do not judge the character
	Never have time for myself	Make time for self
	Always tired	Diet and fitness
	Fear of future	Concentrate on the present
	Always in debt	Get professional advice

This list can be as long as you wish, but you must be honest with yourself. You will find that generally the negative column is always much longer that the positive. The aim is to reverse that. Your life is a work in progress and a constant journey so there will always be aspects in our lives we wish to make better. No matter how perfect life may seem, there is always room for improvement.

Before you go on to the next exercise, get a notebook that can act as a journal for all your goals and plans. Writing down helps us remember powerfully and enables us to see our progress with clarity.

I have had my current journal for seven years. When I look back I never cease to be amazed by how much I have changed.

The visualisation technique allows us to be in the most receptive state to form new dominant thoughts, but it is the exercises whilst being in that state which create the change.

I have sought to keep the exercises as simple as possible, so to avoid being overly descriptive, I have made them as short as possible. The stages are: we enter the deep relaxation state; visualise a favourite place where we are peaceful. We enter a cinema passing people we know as we go. On the screen we see our past. Then we see the present. Then we see the future. We exit and return to our favourite place. Then we count back to full awareness.

The exercise will concentrate on what happens inside the cinema, so before you do a particular exercise, the short notes will guide you and be easy to remember. In the case of changing the negative qualities to positive qualities, the notes would appear like this, which indeed are the exercises to do in this session.

Visualisation Exercise

When you are in the 'Now Showing' part of the visualisation:
See the negative attributes
Freeze the image
Turn it to black and white
Have it fade away.
Then when you visit the 'Coming Soon' screen:
See yourself living the changes you identified in your 'To change from negative to positive' column.

Exercise 2
Behaviours

We show the world what we think of ourselves and others through our behaviours which are seen, felt and heard by ourselves and others.

Behaviours are described in the dictionary as acting or functioning in a particular way. Our behaviours are the 'front' for all that lies beneath and manifest themselves as attitude, feelings, beliefs and thoughts.

It is worth understanding attitude and its impact on behaviour in more detail. This understanding will help you have greater confidence in the visualisation process and clarity as to its importance in your life.

Our beliefs are 'truths' we hold made up from past experiences, external influences, and current perceptions e.g. life is great, life is tough, men are shallow, women can't be trusted, bosses never listen to you, travelling is dangerous and so on. Attitude is how we react to life, based upon our beliefs.

We speak on average 50,000 words inside our heads a day. Make no mistake; your thoughts are driving your life.

It is our thoughts, which give weight to an event or situation, which lace it with emotion, feeling, and put a 'good/bad' judgement upon it and gives it power over us. The thought always comes first. You cannot have a feeling or emotion without first having a thought.

Stuff happens in life which sucks. No one chooses the sad, debilitating, or disappointing. We do not wake up and think 'oh today I will screw up my life and everyone else's'.

When thoughts and emotions go on the rampage, you can be sure you are not the one in the driving seat. Whenever you feel out of control, over-emotional, overly sensitive, it is generally 20% due to the present person or incident and 80% due to past experience and therefore an old emotional 'programme', which is stuck in the same old groove running the same old sounds – controlling you.

To get a winning attitude, the first place you have to take charge is inside your own head so that rampant thoughts and emotions don't hijack you!

An event is just an event. The event in itself has no emotion, feeling, or judgement attached to it.

It rains. A bird sings. A train is late. The car breaks down en route to a hot date.

It is not what happens to us that matters, it is what we do about it that counts.

'Old programmes' run inside your head as persistently as a piece of software once programmed. It will run, and run, and run for as long as you let it – or until you change it.

Focus on the situation, learn to observe it, and choose your response.

This can be any situation where you normally 'respond' without thinking. It may be a slow line in a supermarket, a rude shop assistant, or a cancelled train.

Recognise that your only control is over how you think, feel, and respond. By learning to stay balanced in your emotional response, you are giving yourself control and choices. This will in turn develop assertiveness and confidence.

Either you control how you feel, or how you feel will hijack your response and will control you, leaving you with feelings of guilt, despair and anguish.

Hijacking is when we instantly react to a stimulus. Sometimes it feels like we have not had time to think about it and have no control. It helps to identify what hijacks us to feel unassertive. What is it that pushes your buttons?

In your journal make a list of things over which you have no control that annoy you.

For example:

1. Being stuck in slow moving traffic

2. Rudeness from shop assistants

3. Being caught in bad weather

4. Junk mail

5. People who patronise you

Now that you are aware of what causes you to be hijacked and takes you off the path to successful action, you can make a conscious decision that the next time you face any of the situations you have identified, or a new one that pushes your buttons, you will be able to stay in control and avoid being hijacked. You choose whether it will affect you, or you will affect it. To do this, you only need your self-awareness to recognise when it is happening and that you can control your response.

HEALTH CHECK

How do we know if beliefs are healthy or unhealthy?
   Ask yourself these two simple questions:

   Does this belief take me closer to or further from my goals in life?

   Does it help me to move forward, or does it hold me back in some way?

To change and create your success you must choose the best beliefs, and attitudes to support you in life. Then listen out for signs of negative or damaging chatter and challenge it, question its relevance, and replace it with a more supportive set of language, beliefs, and attitudes, which will produce more constructive and positive emotions and feelings and therefore more productive behaviours.

THE IMPORTANCE OF BELIEF

If you truly believe something, how you talk, how you behave and how you think will all be consistent with that belief.
   If we repeatedly use the same thought we create a strong association and memory.

Imagine that you have won a wonderful prize, and the award ceremony is going to take place in one month's time. You have been told you are going to get the award, you have read the letter confirming it. You have had your hand shaken and your back slapped – everyone has congratulated you. How are you going to feel and act for the remainder of the month? Will you act reticently or nervously? No! Of course not! You will act in a manner that is consistent with that belief and knowledge.

And so it should be with your own future goals.

Believe that they exist in the future, and act accordingly. Your self-belief will manifest itself both in your inner confidence and in your actions.

Since your brain thinks in images, it needs to visualise clearly what it is seeking to achieve.

Every thought and action take us either closer towards our goal, or further from it. Everything has a consequence – cause and effect is the universal law of nature. However in between cause and effect we choose our attitudes based on our beliefs and our feelings.

The new beliefs and attitudes will manifest as new patterns of behaviour that you employ to shape your future. If you want those patterns to continue, you must continue to visualise them until they become automatic and habitual. But if you are not happy with them, then you can have the choice and ability to start the process of change right now. Complacency, indifference and procrastination are your major enemies.

Visualisation Exercise

When you are in the 'Now Showing' part of the visualisation:
See the events which hijack your response
Freeze the image
Turn it to black and white
Have it fade away.
Then when you visit the 'Coming Soon' screen:
See yourself remaining calm and controlled when such an event
  occurs.

Exercise 3
Commitment

Commitment is a massive factor in success, and a faithful companion when the going gets tough. When you commit to a goal, you have to do so with 100% belief that you are going to make it. The commitment switch has two positions: on and off.

Passionate commitment stops successful achievers from ever quitting. It keeps them believing and persevering, no matter how hard the going gets, because they know that in the end they're going to get there. Giving up is not an option.

Sometimes in life no one will believe in you, or what you're doing, or attempting to do. It is at these times that you will need all your strength to keep going, and that is when having a strong, positive self-image helps.

Never mistake a single defeat for final defeat. Never forget that many of the most successful individuals in history have in common the experience of defeat. They have known failure; they have known rock bottom. And what they have all done is picked themselves up, dusted themselves down and started all over again.

Yet many of us find ourselves making the same lack of progress in life that we have often experienced. We tend to give up at the same point, and though we believe that we are committed, in truth we are probably not. What we are is enthusiastic, keen, purposeful and zealous, but we are not committed.

Very often when we look at the mountain tops which represent our long-term goals, they seem too inaccessible, too far away, too steep and with too much risk along the way. Therefore our enthusiasm or zeal is exposed as being just that, an emotion without substance.

To be committed to a goal requires that you believe 100% that you are going to achieve the goal, and take positive action towards the goal every day, no matter what the outcome.

In Part 2 I wrote about a seventy-four mile walk across Scotland, that almost became too much for me after forty-six miles with twenty-eight miles to go. I can still remember the crushing fatigue and knowing if I gave up all the pain would go away. I decided to continue for another 200 yards to a boulder, then I looked 200 yards up the hill and picked another point (or micro-goal).

The reality is that sometimes with the very best intentions in the world, we fail ourselves and give in. This damages our self-image often in a very minor way, but what happens is that we accept giving in more easily in another situation. Obviously there are always situations where we simply do not have a choice, but they are in the minority.

To be committed therefore we have to stay true to the goal at hand. In my case it was 200 yards to a boulder. It may seem small and insignificant, but at that moment I did not believe I could walk twenty-eight miles. As each goal of 200 yards was realised, my confidence grew and my commitment became a determination to keep going.

We all face hardships and for many it marks the point where we gave up, or worse believed we failed.

The purpose of this exercise is to see yourself at the point where in the past you would have given up, and change that image in your mind, to continuing through the challenge. See yourself as heroic, sticking to the goal – persevering through adversity – but just not giving up. Remember success will follow your last failure. We never know when that will be, which is why commitment is for me the key to success.

Visualisation Exercise

When you are in the 'Previously Showing' part of the visualisation:
See the events in your life when you committed to action
See yourself succeeding against hardship
Step into the scene and feel the success, the power, the commitment.
Then when you visit the 'Coming Soon' screen: hear yourself say
  'the power of personal commitment is part of my success'.

Exercise 4
Habit Busting

Many of our behaviours are the result of unconscious patterns of behaviour. These 'bad' habits will prevent you from changing until you consciously change them.

The sadness is how many people just accept these destructive habits, as being somehow beyond their control. They are not. You created them, often unconsciously, and now you are going to uncreate them to replace them with habits which are productive and beneficial.

To do this we need a new blueprint, and that lies at the heart of this exercise. But before we go to the exercise, consider the following: we generally only change our life because of a crisis or events over which we had no control. We have all experienced this either personally or seen others go through it.

The single most important thing I want you to realise is this: people fail to break habits, not because they cannot do so (as they believe and would have you believe too) but because they don't want to. No matter how much they protest to the contrary, they don't want to, and have convinced themselves instead that they can't.

On her twenty-first birthday my mother smoked her first cigarette, and continued to smoke for the next fifty-seven years. At the age of seventy-eight she stopped and has never smoked a cigarette since that day.

It should come as no surprise that there was a big event in her life. She was diagnosed with major heart problems and blockages in her carotid artery. She would require major surgical procedures, which carried a serious risk.

So my mother was told that to give herself the best recovery, and a good future quality of life, she would have to stop smoking. She did.

I spoke to her about previous attempts and past failures. She concluded that even though she tried to stop, she never really wanted to.

I think we too often identify 'bad' habits which keep us from being the person we most want to be, but feel we can do nothing about it. In truth we don't want to change. Our habits are strangely comforting. We like the odd cigarette after dinner, or the relaxing drink when we come home from work, having the rich sauce at dinner, or biting our nails. We continue to do nothing about these habits which don't make us happy in the long-term. Because we don't really want to.

To break these habits, or any habit, you must realise that until you determine to take full responsibility for the effects of your habit, then breaking it will be impossible.

Habit busting is easy once you recognise you have been conning yourself on previous attempts – you believe you gave it your best shot – and it didn't work out, and never will.

Here is some good news – you didn't give it your best shot, not even close. Because when you give it your best shot you will succeed. Because at that moment you will want to change, that belief will give you the understanding that you really can.

Belief before behaviour is a crucial concept – until you believe you can break a habit, a behavioural change alone will almost never be enough. So in the following exercise, see in your mind the 'bad' habits fading away, and being replaced by the 'good' habits. It's that simple.

Visualisation Exercise

When you are in the 'Now Showing' screen:
See the habits in your life that are holding you back
Freeze the picture
Turn it to black and white
Let it fade away.
When you visit the 'Coming Soon' screen: see yourself free of the old habits and hear yourself say 'I got rid of my bad habits. They had no place in my life. I have replaced them with positive success-ful habits which every day move me closer to my goals.'

Exercise 5
Facing Up To Fear

It is natural to be afraid, but if we don't examine our fears we can end up living in a state of fearfulness, spending most of our waking hours worrying about things we have imagined which are never going to happen, or worrying about things over which we have no control.

The two greatest fears in life are failure and rejection.

Understand and accept that failure is something that happens instead of trying to avoid failure at all cost. When you do fail, put it in perspective and look for the lesson to be learned. Do not think of it as evidence that you are a failure, always bound to fail.

Your past failures are events that happened in the past. They are not what you are about; they are not labels that you should stick to yourself and forever identify with. They are events that happened – learn the lesson.

If you go through life vaguely hoping for the best but preparing for the worst, the worst is what you will get. If, on the other hand, you are *determined* to achieve the best, then it is up to you to give yourself every chance to do exactly that.

So how can we control fear, which threatens to get in the way of us achieving our goals?

Again, it is a matter of choice. Remember that you can control your emotions. It is a matter of regaining control by choosing how you are going to think. It takes practice and dedication. Emotions are important; they tell us we are alive. It is equally important to recognise the messages that emotions might be bringing to us.

1. Acknowledge the fear.

2. Feelings demand to be acknowledged and will often calm down once they feel 'heard'. Ask yourself what you can learn from them.

3. Once you have acknowledged the fear, ask yourself, 'is this fear real, or imagined?'

4. If it is real, then exercise awareness and understanding about the nature of the threat. Whatever the fear may be, you will find that learning all about it will enable you to overcome it. You can even get professional counselling if necessary. By gaining knowledge about the subject of your fear, you will deconstruct it. Remember – knowledge liberates, and ignorance imprisons. So trace it, face it – and replace it.

5. If it is an imagined fear, let it go. Acknowledge to yourself both in your visualisation and self-talk that your belief was false. So trace it, face it – and forget it.

Courage is not the absence of fear, it is the ability to face our fears. Recognise that these fears exist mainly in our imaginations. When we face these fears and overcome them, we grow strong on the inside. Create a 'never-quit' personal philosophy and see your fears simply as obstacles you can overcome. When you really want to do something you will find a way – and when you don't you'll find an excuse!

Visualisation Exercise

When you are in the 'Now Showing' screen:
See the fears in your life that are holding you back
Freeze the picture
Turn it to black and white
Let it fade away.
When you visit the 'Coming Soon' screen: see yourself free of those fears and hear yourself say 'The fears in my life that held me back are fading away, I am growing, with courage and knowledge. False fears have no place in my life, I am growing stronger every day.'

Exercise 6
The Inner Coach – Self-Talk

You will doubtless be familiar with the notion of professional athletes who have coaches. The purpose is to build their confidence, plan their training schedule, advise on technique and build up their self-belief, to enable them to win.

There are coaches who have an excellent track record of winning. They seem to be able to get more out of the person or team that they coached than would otherwise have been the case.

The coach communicates with players or athletes by showing them what they want done. They also plan with them how they are going to do it, and put positive thoughts of victory into their heads again and again, by telling them that 'they are going to win'.

Would it not be great to have such a person in your life ten hours a day? This person would:

- help you set goals and plan how to achieve them

- absolutely believe that you can succeed

- motivate you and reinforce your commitment

- show you clearly the right way

- believe in you.

There is – this person is you.

There is a cruel irony that we will give positive encouragement and advice to our friends as they embark on a life change, or personal challenges, yet beat ourself up for small failings and continually give ourselves negative self-talk.

Remember the old saying, 'Garbage In . . . Garbage Out'. If the self-talk you give yourself is negative, then you will be reinforcing those beliefs.

The huge advantage of visualisation is that we directly influence our subconscious minds, and that in turn allows us to change our self-image and patterns of behaviour automatically.

However when we are not visualising, our subconscious mind is still active and processing the information we put into it.

This is the reason that self-talk, and positive affirmations are so critically important on accelerating us to making the changes work.

If our talk is congruent with our new beliefs they become real much more rapidly.

Therefore in this exercise I want you to examine your current use of self-talk. I doubt very much whether you actively think about it.

For many people the idea of self-talk is 'silly' – a grown adult giving themselves praise for the smallest things, and telling themselves they are capable. Whatever your previous opinion, I want to deal with the facts. Positive affirmations and self-talk will build up your self-image, and encourage you to continue to stay committed, motivated and on-plan. Through them, you create your own inner coach who believes in you, wants the best for you, will encourage you to get up every time you fall over, and who helps you to think, walk, talk and act like a winner.

POSITIVE AFFIRMATIONS AND SELF-TALK

Keep it simple and always base it on the present moment. Whatever the subject or situation keep the language positive.

Use short, memorable and easy-to-remember phrases and expressions.

When the situation merits it, use longer self-talks as though you were coaching a friend before they embark on a personal challenge, again always keeping the language simple and positive.

Examples:

I am succeeding

My commitment is total as I move towards my future success

I am changing every day towards personal fulfilment

I am attractive and capable, and shall face every challenge with courage

I shall appreciate the opportunities that today brings

I choose to be positive in all situations, at all times

I am not afraid of failure

Five, ten, fifty or a hundred times a day say them quietly with your inner voice when you are around others, or shout it aloud when you are on your own.

Visualisation Exercise

When you are in the 'Coming Soon' screen:
See yourself having succeeded
Feel the emotions that moment creates for you
Look around the scene and 'be there'
Hear yourself say, 'I have succeeded and continue to grow towards future successes in my life'.
As you 'see' count back from one to ten, returning to full awareness
Repeat the most powerful affirmations from the visualisation.

Exercise 7
Setting Meaningful Goals

Those who succeed in the realisation of their goals are purposeful, passionate, and focused in how they live their lives. They honour themselves by working to reach their true potential.

For most people their goals tend to be 'things'. By things I mean material goals such as a dream job, a perfect home, a holiday, a lifestyle.

Once they have reached that goal, they want a better job, a bigger home, more exotic holidays, a millionaire lifestyle. But sooner or later they become accustomed to these things and in many cases they do not bring the happiness or fulfilment that had been originally anticipated.

I believe that material success is a by-product of personal achievement, and if your goals are not about 'things' but rather about purpose and meaning, then our lives become never ending journeys. In *Natural Born Winners* I wrote that success is not a destination, rather it is an experience of the journey. But a journey to where? In life we need to have a sense of meaning and purpose behind our goals. The achievement of the goal gives us something we desire, and the goal becomes simply an enabler. It is for this reason that when you set a goal it should have a meaning to you that goes beyond personal material or financial reward.

Therefore to be fully engaged in the process of realising your goal, it is important that you are emotionally connected to your goal.

Let's look at two common examples. One is weight loss: if your goal is to lose a surplus 40 lbs, the question you should be asking yourself is not 'I wonder if I can lose 40 lbs?' rather than 'What will losing 40 lbs give me?' It will increase your longevity, reduce your blood pressure, increase your energy and make you feel better about yourself. It is in these aspects that you find your meaning, and in doing so you find purpose, passion and commitment.

The second example is pretty straightforward and realistic. Most people would say that they want to be rich, but rarely do they say (beyond the obvious material rewards) what else it would bring them. In fact it would give them freedom of choice, peace of mind, the means to help others. It would give them the opportunity to develop their interests, travel at will, and help others. If you think of your goals in these terms they come alive.

That is why when you set a goal for yourself you examine the meaning and purpose behind it.

So when you set your goals, in addition to asking yourself is it realistic, ask yourself: is there meaning behind it?

Visualisation Exercise

When you are in the 'Coming Soon' screen see the goals you have set being realised
See also what these goals enable you to do
Step into the scene you have created
Recognise the meaning that lies behind your goals
See the joy that this brings you
Hold strongly in the scene the purpose and meaning that lies behind your goals
Say to yourself: 'Achieving my goals enables me to . . .'
Keep that thought in your mind whenever you think of your goal.

Exercise 8
Creating Your Plan For Success

As I mentioned earlier in the book, your plan is a road map that guides you to your final goal. You determine the timeframe and the short- and medium-term goals that have to be achieved along the way. You would be amazed how many people do not have goals. You would be equally surprised to discover how many people have goals but no plans.

Your plan becomes your blueprint for action.

Creating a written plan of action will enable you to measure accurately your progress and take actions to move yourself in the direction of your goal. You will experience more apparent coincidences because you will recognise opportunities as your subconscious mind is continually seeking to bring the visualised goal to life, and consequently recognises events that will assist.

In your journal:

Write each goal on a separate page.

Determine the date by which you want to achieve this goal.

Now work back from that date and identify the goals and achievement dates for each of them.

Continue to do this until you have identified your first twenty-four hour goal.

Each goal will require that you take action. As you study the goal, you will be able to identify the challenges that you are likely to face. Once you have identified the challenges and likely barriers, it becomes possible to find ways to overcome them. The knowledge you need to acquire and the strategies you need to employ can now be planned.

Studies have shown that people who have clear goals and a written plan experience more success in achieving their goals than those who do not.

It is a common mistake to imagine that the goal is enough and the plan need not be written down. How many people when asked where the information is, proudly tap their head and announce 'It's all up there'? It may well all be up there, but you really need to be able to see it in black and white, to chart your progress against your planned timeframe. Of all the reasons why people seem to fail, the lack of a **clear** plan, is top. Vague ideas, or temporary initiatives are not plans, so if it is not written down, with measurable steps and a timeframe, then you don't have a plan.

For me the greatest use of a plan is that it allows me to work out in the smallest detail what needs to be done.

When I go on holiday, depending on what I wish to experience, I do one of two things. I either plan in detail every hour of the trip, even building in free time just to explore. I end up with a detailed itinerary – every eventuality planned for, every ticket purchased and all accommodation booked. On the other hand, at other times I want to recapture that sense of adventure I experienced as a student hitchhiking through Europe, not knowing where I would end up the next day. I have bought tickets to cities, and landed with no plan other than to go where my fancy took me.

The former holiday is always more rewarding because the planning gives me focus and direction. The unplanned holidays, lacking focus and direction, have some highlights, but much of the time is spent trying to organise myself.

So it is in our lives that the more we plan clearly in advance, the better we will use our time. The more focused will be our actions, and the more rewarding the journey.

The only difference between your life and a holiday is that your life is infinitely more rewarding and meaningful than any holiday could ever be.

Please don't leave it to chance.

Visualisation Exercise

When you are in the 'Coming Soon' room

See yourself as having succeeded

Feel the joy of that moment

Hear youself say 'I have succeeded in achieving my goals through commitment to my plan'

In the moment of future success be aware that the success was not accidental, recognise it was planned, and say to yourself 'My success was not luck it was planned'

As you count back from one to ten

Returning to full awareness

Hold the thought that your success was the result of planning and not luck.

Conclusion

When The Going Gets Tough, Remember...

Within every person there is the memory of a child who succeeded very early in life, who for a short time believed that anything was possible. To this child, there were no barriers and no thoughts of status, height or colour.

Life is a work in progress and sometimes the going gets tough. Let the negative times simply wash over you and remember they will pass.

You were born with an inherent capacity to be a winner. See yourself as a winner, because every victory along the way, no matter how small, will give you the confidence to go on to greater su___ss.

Believe that no matter how often you fall down, you will ___ one more time. This is your life and your journey, focus ___ you want and not on what you don't want. Do not be d' ___ by setbacks or negative opinions.

Taking the first step can seem frightening and hard. But take it anyway, no matter how small, because it is that step that will start you on your journey to whatever goal you have set yourself. Whatever happens, it will move you forward in your life and you will never regret it.

Create a 'can do' image of yourself that becomes fixed in your subconscious.

Always do your best to do your best.

Celebrate each and every success you have, no matter how small. It will reinforce your self-image as being successful.

We are born without prejudice and without any sense of externally imposed limits on our potential. The limiting beliefs you learned in the past can be unlearned, by following the advice in this book.

When you finally get to your destination, it won't be the pain or the hardship or the setbacks that you remember. It will be the satisfaction of having done what you set out to do, with the certain knowledge that a lifetime of future success awaits you.

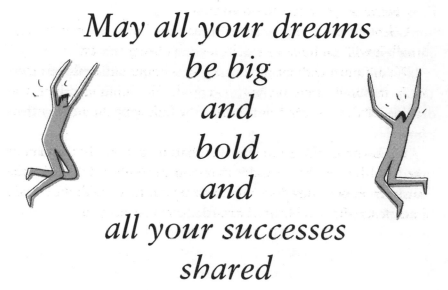

*May all your dreams
be big
and
bold
and
all your successes
shared*

ROBIN SIEGER

Robin Sieger is the founder of Sieger International Ltd with offices in London (UK), and Charlotte NC (USA). The company has built an international reputation amongst businesses as a powerful catalyst for performance transformation.

Sieger International helps individuals and organisations release their potential through the creation of a success culture, turning potential into profit. It has a wide range of clients – from start-up entrepreneurs through to FTSE 100 companies.

In addition to the business arena, Sieger International runs the 100% NBW™ programme for schools enabling children to develop their self-worth and inspire them to learn and apply the principles behind personal success.

An acknowledged world class keynote speaker, Robin Sieger is noted for his humour and his ability to inspire, motivate, and transform audiences around the world. He was one of the first three speakers in the UK to be awarded a fellowship in recognition of his achievements. His corporate training, consulting and speaking clients include British Airways, British Telecom, General Motors, Ford Motor Co., HSBC, IBM, Microsoft, McDonald's, Nokia, Coca-Cola and Zurich Financial.

Natural Born Winners has been sold in over sixty countries worldwide and in 2004 was turned into a television series.

FOR FURTHER INFORMATION ON
ROBIN SIEGER AND SIEGER
INTERNATIONAL LTD'S TRAINING
AND CONSULTING SERVICES, PLEASE
CONTACT:

Sieger International Ltd
Molasses House
Plantation Wharf
London SW11 3TH

0845 2305400

www.sicgcrinternational.com

robin@siegerinternational.com

Perfect People Skills

Andrew Floyer Acland

Perfect People Skills helps you to deal with other people effectively and how to be aware of your own behaviour too. Differences of direction and motivation, personality, ethnic group, gender, class and ability can all bring problems, as well as those presented by 'difficult types'. The author provides some powerful ideas for preventing people problems, resolving conflict and building harmonious home and workplaces.

The book is comprehensive and yet concise and to-the-point. It is written in simple, clear language and is designed to be of immediate, practical benefit to readers in developing better relationships at work and outside work.

Chapters include:

Grounding	Listening
Questioning	Empathising
Speaking	Negotiating
Proposing	Counselling
Confronting	Preventing

arrow books

Perfect Presentation

Andrew Leigh and Michael Maynard

More and more people find they are asked to give formal presentations to colleagues or clients as part of their everyday job. And not surprisingly many people are apprehensive at the prospect. This book provides a thorough – but friendly – guide to making successful, professional presentations. The book is comprehensive, and yet concise and to the point. It is written in simple clear language and is designed to be of immediate, practical benefit to readers.

Chapters include:

- Why we need presentation skills
- Basic principles
- The 5 'P's of Perfect Presentations
  - ➤ *Preparation*
  - ➤ *Purpose*
  - ➤ *Presence*
  - ➤ *Passion*
  - ➤ *Personality*
- Trouble Shooting
- Team Presentations

arrow books

Perfect Leader

Andrew Leigh and Michael Maynard

The perfect guide to unleashing your leadership potential

Are leaders born or made? *Perfect Leader* shows clearly how everybody can learn to exercise leadership. The book is comprehensive, yet concise and to the point. It is written in clear language and is designed to be of immediate, practical benefit to readers. It explains exactly what it takes to be a leader by identifying and examining the seven 'I's of leadership:

Insight
Initiative
Inspiration
Involvement
Improvisation
Individuality
Implementation

Today's business methods, with their emphasis on teamwork, and on fewer layers of management, mean that there is a need for effective leaders to bring about corporate success – and in the process build themselves a satisfying career.

The authors Andrew Leigh and Michael Maynard run Maynard Leigh Associates, the human resources and development consultancy.

arrow books

Perfect CV

Max Eggert

Whether you're applying for your first job or planning an all-important career move, your CV is the most potent strike weapon in your armoury. This classic, bestselling book is a concise and invaluable guide that gives you the blueprint for the perfect CV. It shows you clearly and quickly how to present you and your skills and experience in the best possible way – and how to avoid the many easily-made mistakes which swiftly antagonize potential employers.

Chapters include:

- What to include – and exclude
- Structures that work for you
- Making your CV say 'see me'
- Presenting yourself in a unique way
- Creating the right image
- 50 tips and strategies

arrow books

Perfect Assertiveness

Jan Ferguson

Perfect Assertiveness helps you to understand more about assertiveness and aggression, and teaches you to understand more about yourself, the possibilities of change and the potential for improvement in personal, social, family and workplace relationships.

Chapters include:

- What does assertiveness really mean?
- Non-assertive behaviour and its results
- What's in it for you?
- You're in charge
- Learn to be your own best friend
- Moving on, letting go
- Handling conflict
- Being an assertive customer
- Setting boundaries and saying 'no'
- Steps to becoming more assertive

Jan Ferguson is an independent trainer, consultant and counsellor working in the field of interpersonal skills.

arrow books

**Order further Arrow titles from your local bookshop,
or have them delivered direct to your door by Bookpost**

☐	**Perfect Counselling** Max Eggert	1 84 413156 4	£6.99
☐	**Perfect People Skills**		
	Andrew Floyer Acland	1 84 413151 3	£6.99
☐	**Perfect Career** Max Eggert	1 84 413145 9	£6.99
☐	**Perfect Interview** Max Eggert	1 84 413143 2	£6.99
☐	**Perfect CV** Max Eggert	1 84 413144 0	£6.99
☐	**Perfect Leader** Leigh and Maynard	1 84 413147 5	£6.99
☐	**Perfect Time Management** Ted Johns	1 84 413157 2	£6.99
☐	**Perfect Business Plan** Ron Johnson	1 84 413148 3	£6.99
☐	**Perfect Presentation**		
	Leigh and Maynard	1 84 413020 7	£6.99
☐	**Perfect Negotiation** Gavin Kennedy	1 84 413149 1	£6.99
☐	**Perfect Assertiveness** Jan Ferguson	1 84 413148 3	£6.99
☐	**Perfect Customer Care** Ted Johns	1 84 413153 X	£6.99

Free post and packing
Overseas customers allow £2 per paperback
Phone: 01624 677237
Post: Random House Books
c/o Bookpost, PO Box 29, Douglas, Isle of Man IM99 1BQ
Fax: 01624 670923
email: bookshop@enterprise.net
Cheques (payable to Bookpost) and credit cards accepted

Prices and availability subject to change without notice.
Allow 28 days for delivery.
When placing your order, please state if you do not wish to receive any
additional information.
www.randomhouse.co.uk/arrowbooks

a r r o w   b o o k s